Professors
as
Teachers

KENNETH E. EBLE

Professors as Teachers

Jossey-Bass Publishers
San Francisco • Washington • London • 1973

FIRST EDITION
First printing: February 1972
Second printing: July 1972
Third printing: October 1973

Code 7202

The Jossey-Bass
Series in Higher Education

*A report of the
Project to Improve College Teaching
sponsored by the
American Association of University Professors and
the Association of American Colleges
and funded by the Carnegie Corporation.
The views expressed are not presented as
those of the sponsoring or funding organizations.*

Preface

Professors as Teachers has grown out of my work with the Project to Improve College Teaching. This project, developed during the 1968–1969 academic year, was sponsored by the American Association of University Professors and the Association of American Colleges. Funding for a two-year period was provided by the Carnegie Corporation. The funded proposal had three objectives: to study the recognition and evaluation of teaching, the career development of effective college teachers, and the development of optimum working conditions for effective teaching.

Financing of the project provided for a full-time director and secretary and maintenance of a project office, various conferences associated with specific objectives, the commissioning of a study of optimum working conditions, and funds for travel, publications and other means of furthering the project's work. Close cooperation with the AAUP and the AAC were maintained throughout the life of the project. In the course of the project's work, I tried to become conversant with published material related to the objectives of the project and to explore the general subject of college teaching. Two aspects have been discussed in detail in *The Recognition and Evaluation of Teaching* and *Career Development of the Effective College Teacher*, published by the project and distributed through the national office of the American Association of University Professors. A final conference in Santa Fe addressed the general problem of renewing undergraduate teaching. A shortened version of the background paper for that conference, "The Teaching Environment," by Jerry Gaff and Robert Wilson, appeared in the *AAUP Bulletin*, Winter 1971, and is available as a reprint.

The project owes a great debt to the hundreds of faculty members, students, and administrators who contributed both substance and encouragement to our work. Individuals who took part in various conferences connected with the project's work are especially to be thanked. It is appropriate to thank members of the two sponsoring associations who have strongly supported and will continue to support our efforts. All of us associated with the project are grateful to the Carnegie Corporation for providing financial support.

It is not possible to acknowledge by names the individuals on many campuses and in organizations concerned with higher education who invited me to visit or who responded to my requests for information. The list of campuses visited acknowledges these debts and indicates the extent of these visits. The universities include Alabama, Arizona, Auburn, Ball State, British Columbia, California at Santa Cruz, Central Michigan, Cincinnati, Colorado, Colorado State, Columbia, Dayton, Delaware, Florida, Hartford, Harvard, Kentucky, Maryland, Massachusetts, Minnesota, Missouri at Kansas City, Nevada, New Mexico, New Mexico State, North Carolina at Greensboro, Ohio, Oregon, Princeton, Southern Methodist, Tennessee, Texas Christian, Texas at Austin, Texas at Arlington, Texas at El Paso, Toledo, Utah, Washington, Western Michigan, Wichita State, and Wisconsin; state and liberal arts colleges—Central Washington, Coe, Coppin State, Loretto Heights, Marymount (N.Y.), Notre Dame (Md.), Oakland (Mich.), Occidental, Park (Mo.), Portland State, St. John's (Santa Fe), St. Mary of the Plains, Salve Regina, San Diego State, Southern Oregon, Swarthmore, Towson State, V.M.I., Wake Forest, Washington and Lee, Western Maryland, Western Washington, Wofford, and the University of Albuquerque; community or junior colleges—Catonsville (Md.), Flat-

Preface

head Valley (Mont.), Foothill (Calif.), Laramie County (Wyo.), Montgomery (Md.), and Skagit Valley (Wash.).

I would like to single out the following people for special thanks for their consistent encouragement of college teaching over the years and for specific help during the period of the project: Robert Helbling and Edward Lueders, University of Utah; Benjamin DeMott, Amherst; E. J. Shoben, Jr., Evergreen College; L. Shelbert Smith, Central State University; Ruth Eckert, University of Minnesota; and Merrimon Cunningm and Robert Rankin of the Danforth Foundation.

Finally, I am deeply grateful to the administrators, faculty members, and student who made up the advisory board: Robert Van Waes, AAUP; John Gillis, AAC; Bruce Dearing, State University of New York at Binghamton; Edward Eddy, Chatham College; Winston Ehrmann, Cornell College; Harry Gideonse, New School for Social Research; Wilbert McKeachle, University of Michigan; Neill Megaw, University of Texas; Rosemary Pierrel, Pembroke College; Jim Sutton, University of Iowa; and Henry T. Yost, Amherst. While they gave me full freedom to pursue my inquiries, they also provided a ready source of planning, advice, and encouragement.

Salt Lake City
January 1972

Kenneth E. Eble

Contents

Contents

Professors
as
Teachers

CHAPTER 1

Professors in the Classroom

$\blacklozenge\!\!\times\!\!\blacklozenge\!\!\times\!\!\blacklozenge\!\!\times\!\!\blacklozenge\!\!\times\!\!\blacklozenge\!\!\times\!\!\blacklozenge\!\!\times\!\!\blacklozenge\!\!\times\!\!\blacklozenge\!\!\times\!\!\blacklozenge$

Any critic of teaching should have, as his basic credentials, the experience of sitting in many classes of many teachers through many long hours. That is not the whole of teaching, by any means, but it is the basic experience that provides the proper beginning of reflective thought about teaching. Students have this experience, and that alone makes them appropriate critics, often severe critics, of teachers and teaching.

From 1969 to 1971 I visited many classes on many campuses. During the same period I spent much time talking with students and faculty and administrators about college teaching. I describe here teaching in undergraduate classes as I have observed it. I do not purport to have sampled college teaching adequately, either in number of observations or in careful selection of a representative sample. But I do promise to be honest in reporting what I saw and to be temperate in drawing conclusions.

To begin, a word about my method, such as it was. I spent the first three months as director of the project planning ways to carry out the objectives outlined in the Preface. The first step was to inform members of the higher education community—people at

1

two- and four-year colleges and undergraduate colleges within universities—of the project's aims. Responses from an initial short questionnaire, sent to five hundred deans, led directly to my visits to campuses. Of the three parts of the project—evaluation of teaching, career development of effective teachers, and development of optimum working conditions—the evaluation of teaching clearly provoked the most interest. Out of that interest and particularly out of the activities of students in registering or wishing to register opinions on courses and teaching, I began to receive invitations to visit various schools. The invitations came from colleges sufficiently diverse to provide an adequately random sampling, though I did arrange to visit specific colleges to widen the range of my experience.

The list of colleges I visited may be found in the Preface. The number reached seventy in forty states and included small and large, impoverished and affluent, public and private, private under a variety of supporting boards, rural and urban, traditional and innovative, two-year community college, and national university. The time I spent on any one campus was short, one or at most two days (with the exception of the University of Utah, where I have been teaching and observing for fifteen years). I did not visit classes at every school, and at a few schools I did not have much direct contact with students. I did engage in discussions with individuals, small groups, or large groups at all schools, and these discussions included students, faculty, and members of the administration.

Visits to classes were not as easy to arrange as I thought they would be. My first impulse was to visit classes of teachers identified as superior and to supplement these visits with personal interviews. I regret that the other demands of the project made this impossible. I think the job needs to be done, preferably by a college teacher possessing many of the characteristics of a good journalist and accompanied by a skilled cameraman. I next tried for a random sample of teaching as it was going on during my campus visits. This attempt also posed some difficulties, for I was sensitive to faculty reluctance to have a stranger drop in on a class, and both students and administrators were inclined toward identifying "best" teachers (or under some provocation, "worst"). As it became apparent that limited visiting was all I could do, I tried to

2

find a student on each campus to pass me off as some mildly strange uncle who wanted to see the student's professors in action. This did not work either. Even students I knew wanted to steer me to the fellow who was "really fantastic," or when I put my finger on a name in the catalog, they might say, "You don't want that one. He's a real bummer."

The method I settled on and used most often during the second year was to scan the class schedule, pick out kinds of classes, and see whether visits could be arranged. In some instances, I found it possible to wander around campus and slip into a large lecture class without catching the attention of either students or teacher. In many ways, I preferred that kind of visit, even though it violated my own precept that I would not visit unless invited. I do not think my presence was detected, and, detected or not, I apologize to those individual professors whose privacy I violated. Nor do I blame professors for being reluctant to invite visitors, though I think it is better for learning to regard teaching as a public activity than to regard the classroom as the professor's castle.

There are many faults to be found in my method. Teaching is probably not quite the same when one is being observed as when one is not. But the teaching which suffered by my presence may have been offset by the extra care and preparation that went into some classes when the teacher knew he was going to have a visitor. What I was after was a glance at different teachers and classes as they went on day after day. At the least, the teachers I visited constituted a largely unselected and diverse sample; the classes I attended embraced a range of subject matters, levels, sizes, and methods of instruction.

What are the general conclusions I draw from this round of visits? I have divided my observations into two parts, the first four having to do with the conduct of classes and the last six leading to generalizations about attitudes toward teaching. I save discussion of the latter group for Chapter Two.

First, classroom teaching is still largely a matter of a single professor talking to, presenting material to, fairly large numbers of students. Despite the innovative practices to be found on almost every campus, the dominant mode of instruction remains the lecture or lecture-discussion given on a regular basis to numbers of students ranging from ten or fifteen to many hundreds. The pervasiveness of this form can be gathered from the course description booklets put out by students at hundreds of colleges and universities.

At Rutgers, for example, beginning with the students' description of art history and going through English, class sizes range from one thousand to seventeen (though large classes have sections of twenty-five to fifty). Of forty-two courses in art, biology, chemistry, economics, and English, only two departed noticeably from some variant of lecture, lecture-laboratory, or lecture-discussion. (Both exceptions followed the case-study method.) In English and economics, however, discussion was at least as important as lecture, and pure lecture courses, unsupported by laboratory, quiz, or discussion sections, were rare.[1]

At Johns Hopkins, the formal lecture was much more dominant. The students' comments on some of the courses listed—biology through English—give this view:[2]

> lectures were fairly well organized but boring

> lecturer, although he usually knew what he was talking about, . . . was often disorganized and sometimes had very poor presentation delivery

> lectures weak in order and organization (lab course is one of the better courses)

> four lectures per week are scheduled

> lectures are complete, clear, and concise . . . welcome questions

> two levels of presentation . . . book and lectures . . . homework and tests

> well-prepared lectures

> a teacher, unlike most lecturers

> obvious weaknesses . . . lack of discussion sessions

[1] Rutgers College Student Government Association, "Course and Professor Evaluation" (New Brunswick, N.J., Spring 1969), pp. 1–46.
[2] "The Course Guide" (Baltimore, Md.: The Johns Hopkins University, April 1969), pp. 1–12.

class sessions devoted to analysis of ideas

lectures well prepared and organized . . . little time for adequate discusion

lectures interspersed with pertinent and interesting questions

brilliant lecturer

very interesting lecturer

lectures considered worthwhile

informal lecture and discussion

There is little point in going on with this evidence, for the yield is much the same. Class sizes do vary from the small school to the large universities, and to some degree discussion seems to have a better chance at the small school. But in small schools and large, a student can count on spending a great deal of time listening to his professors.

Lecture courses, individual lectures, can be good or bad. Despite a general student dislike of lecturing, a skillful lecturer seems to gain as favorable a response from students as the skillful seminar leader. Classroom teachers do adapt their lectures to their subject matter. The lecture-discussion, for example, appears more often in economics and English than in biology or chemistry, and general lecture sessions in the sciences emphasize basic information and theory, while laboratory sections give students a chance to apply theory and techniques. The lecture can still be defended as a means of conveying information, and conveying information is at least a partial objective of many college courses. One cannot condemn the lecture method out of hand, particularly as the student's total college experience affords such common but varied teaching-learning experiences as drill and recitation, guided reading, discussion, case study, field work, and tutorials, each of which may involve the teacher in a variety of ways.

But having made this defense, I cannot be faithful to my experiences in various classrooms without expressing some strong reservations about the effectiveness of the lecture method. Wherever the student goes during his collegiate years, he is likely to have in-

5

formation and ideas thrust upon him. Some lectures repeat what he is getting in more lucid form in textbooks. Others thrust ideas at the student in ways he must accept even when the lecturer permits discussion or makes a point of entertaining questions. A great many lectures, probably the majority, have little meaning for the student beyond the classrooms and class contexts in which they take place.

To supplement my own observations, let me draw upon two different observations of classroom teaching, made twenty years apart. Paul Klapper, then president emeritus of Queens College, spent two to three weeks at each of six large universities just after World War II. He spent three-fourths of his time visiting classes. His sketch of a fairly representative class is worth repeating here, both for what it reveals about classroom teaching and for comparison with more recent observations.[3]

The course. Introductory economics, three lectures, one recitation weekly.

Grade. A freshman-sophomore course.

Size of class. About 650–700; floor and gallery of large auditorium well filled.

Subject of the hour. Relation of the Federal Reserve Bank to some functions of local banks.

Method. Lecture, with an occasional question to the entire auditorium calling for a one-word answer—"yes, no, 4 per cent, Chicago," etc. Outline on board was placed there before class arrived but could not be read by at least 60 per cent of the audience because the board and hence the writing were too small.

The Instructor. An effective speaker; voice, mannerisms, and occasional questions in lieu of declarative statements are all designed to keep a group listening. His illustrations were simple, concrete, and taken from prevailing local activities. He repeated the same ideas frequently, but the adequacy of his vocabulary made each repetition sound different. The instructor is an experienced hand and has probably been giving these lectures for

[3] "The Professional Preparation of the College Teacher," *Journal of General Education*, April 1949, *3*, 228–244.

years. The material *may* be in mimeographed form peddled openly or surreptitiously by enterprising students.

Student reaction. The class began with a cheer; evidently the instructor is a tradition on the campus. At the beginning all were quiet, but even after the first few minutes evidence of inattention was obvious. Some read a text, some *the* text, some a newspaper, others the student paper. Here and there students did nothing but gaze drowsily into the air. Only one out of three took any notes. In the second half of the hour, there was considerable conversation, orderly to be sure. Many seemed confused by such terms as "custodianship of reserves," "rediscount," "commercial paper," "retain liquid condition," while others looked and wrote as if they knew these business terms.

General Comment. This lecturer is undoubtedly one of the best that one is likely to hear on a university campus. Nevertheless, there was little evidence that he understood that teaching should result in an interplay of mind on mind; that a class hour should be for the student an active hour; that the instructor should contribute something—the fruit of his scholarship and experience—which the students cannot obtain for themselves by their own reading.

More recent observations are those of Conrad Balliet, an associate professor of English at Wittenberg University. In the winter of 1970, Balliet spent a sabbatical leave observing teaching in forty different classes in twenty-five colleges in California. These visits were restricted to English, but English classes account for an important part of many undergraduate programs. I do not draw upon Balliet's observations of individual classes but quote a passage which gives overall impressions and observations.[4]

I . . . sought innovative and creative teachers. In my own past teaching (especially on normal, uninspired days) and from a number of recent inspiring books on teaching, I would like to believe that there is a better approach than the traditional lecture-discussion. I tried to make this position clear when I asked students, chairmen, and administrators who the innovative professors were, yet repeatedly when I got in a classroom of the

[4] "Impressions of Changes," unpublished manuscript (Springfield, Ohio: Wittenberg University, 1970).

7

supposedly best professors on campus, I found a flamboyant lecturer or a congenial soul or a brilliant academician. Not that there is anything wrong with these: I was looking for something different. Regardless of course or curriculum, however, one conclusion seems clear: when we professors get into a classroom, we profess. I found an occasionally effective use of media, or multimedia (the latter a redundant but common expression). Though not particularly new, such media as movies, television and videotape, slides, sound, and theater are still so seldom used in college classes that their effective use struck me as novel. The only significant innovation in the teaching-learning process I found was in the use of affective learning. The terms for the processes involved are various, confusing, and subject to misconception and distortion. Other words used are confluent or congruent education, sensitivity, T-group, encounter, and group dynamics. This approach may not be new, at least in California, but its extensive and intensive use in higher education is comparatively new. And it is the only new approach that engaged the student more actively in the learning process and kept the professor from doing most of the talking.

Balliet's observations square with my own. Innovative teaching can be found if one looks for it, but it constitutes very little of the total experience of a college student. Courses are easier to change than are teaching techniques. The professor giving out, the students maybe taking in, is the central way college teaching takes place. In teaching some subjects, the professor may consciously adopt the discursive mode or respond to the current interest in affective learning, but the classes I visited can be described much as Klapper described the ones he visited after World War II.

Balliet's hope for something better than the lecture-discussion—"I was looking for something different"—is echoed by many college teachers and by a good many more than have found something different or are practicing it if they have. The lecture-discussion as yet so fits the whole structure of higher education that modifications of it are more likely than is setting it aside altogether. The professor's training, the reward structure, and the conflicting claims on his time make the lecture the most common mode of instruction at any given time for almost any teacher. In my visits I encountered very little teaching which did not fit this pattern. And although discussion is in favor just now as a method of instruction, discussion classes were often no more skillfully handled than were lectures. Here are a number of my own observations about classes and teachers.

A discussion class in philosophy. This is a night class, the students a more varied mixture than in day classes, the classroom dirtier, the atmosphere more relaxed. The instructor, in his thirties, is committed to the discussion method.

Class begins with the teacher posing a basic proposition: "There are some questions that can't be resolved scientifically." The teacher may have a fairly clear idea of the importance of the proposition and the ideas the discussion should bring forth, but he does not give much sense of direction to the class. The discussion is fitfully interesting, but as it goes on, students show signs of impatience. Time is going by with apparently too little return.

Sometimes the discussion becomes a private conversation between the teacher and individual students. The teacher tends to withhold clarification, to defer answering questions to some later time. At a crucial point, a student waves his hand and blurts out, "Can anyone tell us just where the hell we are?" The teacher fields the question well, lectures momentarily to give some degree of clarification. The discussion ends with some sense of the loose ends having been brought together.

The next day I attended the same course taught by a different teacher to several hundred students in a large auditorium. The teacher supplemented his lecture presentation by using a slide projector which flashed words like "Lucretius," and "atomism" on a big screen. In my judgment, the class was less successful than the one the night before. While that class had suffered from the students' anxiety that it was not going anywhere, this one suffered from the fact that the students had no reason to care whether it did. What was worse, the instructor was not necessary at all. A taped performance synchronized with the slides would have done as well.

Eighteenth-century literature. This is a survey course, but the teacher, to judge from this example, is not ruled by a necessity to survey. The subject today: *Tristram Shandy.*

The teacher is a young, good-looking woman in a striped

9

turtleneck and red slacks. She sits behind the desk, but increasingly, as the class goes on, she projects more life and movement than a sitting posture often suggests. She obviously has the class with her, uses the students' responses, asks and answers questions very well. Face, hands are alive and expressive. Reads occasionally from book, is extremely good at dramatizing lines.

She seems to have some clear and important objectives in mind: to have the students read the book, to find their interest and pleasure in it enhanced by the discussion, to enlarge their awareness of certain ideas and attitudes which the author is expressing, and to suggest that the book relates to other eighteenth-century literature.

After class I thanked her for a very good hour and asked where she acquired her teaching technique. Her answer was modest and evasive, suggesting that her skill was just something she had acquired along the way. Later, when I talked to her at length, she revealed more to it than that. She had come into teaching directly from a major graduate school with the lecture as her general approach. In the few years she had been teaching, she had become increasingly dissatisfied with the lecture method. On her own and in talks with a like-minded colleague, she began to develop an effective style. Her teaching, on the basis of that one day's observation, seemed to have moved naturally and highly successfully from the presentational to the discursive mode and to draw upon the strengths of each. As a footnote, this teacher later received the department nomination as an outstanding teacher and was officially recognized as such by the Modern Language Association. She did not, however, gain a promotion from assistant to associate professor. The experience did not embitter her, but it left some doubt in her mind about the value her school in fact attached to superior teaching.

Studio course in painting. (I include this example because it is a kind of teaching quite different from lecture-discussion and is confined essentially to the fine arts and athletics.) The instructor is casual, surrounded almost entirely by women, in a studio with easels for about a dozen students. Though the class has a formal period of time set aside, students arrive at different times, many stay after, technique is conversational, with the teacher moving from student to student, raising specific questions about a student's work, giving suggestions, not often illustrating.

Everything seems to depend on the confidence of student in teacher and the teacher's skill in this form of tutoring. All the students seem genuinely engrossed in their work. The instructor appears to have both a personal and a professional interest in them, and they seem responsive to his suggestions. To a higher degree than in most courses, the teacher's effectiveness may be judged by the quality of the student's work. And yet, I still have reservations. How much of what the student does as a painter is due to the teacher and how much to the ability of the student before he ever entered the class?

As my visits were coming to an end, I began to reflect on how campus structures themselves support the lecture method. Some classrooms still have bolted-down seats, and the arm for taking notes is as conspicuous a feature of classroom furniture as the raised speaker's platform and the lectern. In my own appearances on campus, I wanted to be involved in give and take with the audience, but invariably I found myself facing the microphone and podium and very often (since presumably talking about teaching should attract vast audiences) formal stage and auditorium. The newer buildings are changing in this respect. Colleges with different ideas about instruction—St. John's College at Santa Fe, for example—build seminar rooms and student centers with an abundance of small spaces which invite people to sit down and talk. But over most campuses which have to live with their past physical structures hangs an atmosphere which preserves a somewhat anachronistic mode of communicating the results of scholarship. We should not have to be badgered by the young or the media to become aware of this. Changes in our style of learning are to be found everywhere in society. There is no reason why the colleges and universities, whose business is learning, should be the last to respond to change.

Second, textbooks, notes, and the well-stuffed mind are the most widely used audio-visual devices. In this age the means of teaching outdistance any one teacher's ability to use them. Perhaps

11

that is why we hear so much criticism of higher education for failing to take full advantage of technology.

Not a tenth of the technological possibilities were employed in the classrooms I visited. Admittedly, in some institutions whole phalanxes of courses are turned over to closed-circuit television instruction, and language labs and listening posts in the library exist on many campuses. Extremely sophisticated (and expensive) equipment is a first requirement in the sciences and engineering, some of it employed in teaching. But not a great deal more can be added. There is current talk about whole campuses turning to computer-assisted or individualized programed instruction. Community colleges, particularly, look with great favor on such possibilities. But the promises, like those made about interplanetary travel or learning to play the piano by ear, stop short of fulfillment. Technology does not promise to revolutionize learning and teaching. At most, it offers a series of changes which have already modified the behavior of students within learning situations and which have altered in various ways the learning situation itself.

The employment of television in instruction is a good illustration. In the early 1960s, a visitor to college campuses could not have escaped being shown the closed-circuit setup. Today, such instruction is not brought forth as an example of effective teaching. Part of the reason is that televised instruction has become commonplace, and part is that television instruction is probably neither better nor worse than ordinary live instruction. Research shows that for lectures, television instruction results in about the same measurable student accomplishments as does lecturing by live professors to large numbers of students. It meets with acceptance from students and faculty as well as resistance. What the years of working with it have shown is that for some things—demonstrations, presentation of visual materials, close-ups of experiments, for example—it is clearly superior if only because more students can see what is going on and because it enables schools to use off-campus resources of various kinds. Experience seems to place televised instruction with other adjuncts to learning. It is an easier form of film which is most effective as an aid to teaching rather than as the entire method of presentation. Keep in mind that this applies only to television within classroom contexts; it says little about the teaching and learning possibilities which educational programing may have in the home. On campus, television instruction has not revolutionized anything. By now, it has been absorbed into the instructional patterns; it is more powerful, useful, and expensive than lantern slides but still dependent upon teacher and student for its use and its usefulness.

But the academic community has probably neither sufficiently pondered nor tried to adapt to the many changes in everyone's learning which are taking place off campus. Television has probably made an impact here, and that impact is being slowly recognized on campus in a loosening of formal classroom structures; in the demand for wider, more actual experience than the campus provides; in the stress upon affective as well as cognitive learning. An interesting illustration is the attempt to use an excellent video taped course in introductory physics as a campus class. The show had been a great success on *Sunrise Semester* and had the resources for finding and using demonstration equipment few campuses could duplicate. It was taught by an outstanding physicist and an extraordinary teacher. Notwithstanding, the class on campus did not hold student interest, with the result that the physics department had to prepare its own live show along the same lines but with a much higher degree of apparent success. Part of what happened here, I think, resulted from the conditioning television had already subjected students to. Why should they pay tuition, fight for a parking place, sit in a large room with hundreds of other students to get the same thing they could get by turning a knob on their home television sets?

What I have said about television could be said about films, filmstrips, slides, tape recorders, record players, even about posters, diagrams, displays, and books. All are adjuncts to the teacher, and all remain dependent upon the teacher's will and competence. The book has had five hundred years to make the lecture obsolete. It is neither the recalcitrance of professors nor the massive solidity of institutions which has kept that from happening. It is, rather, some recognition of the public, yet personal, nature of teaching. The book is personal but private. The lecture is personal and public. And if we think in terms of instructing a public, we are drawn to use both.

The personal remains important in teaching, perhaps too important, both for those who want to push the teacher off the podium and get him down where everyone learns together and for those who see the personal standing in the way of the endlessly reproducible electronic image. The two are somewhat related, for in the developing theory of the teacher as the facilitator of individual learning, the teacher's direct personal impact actually diminishes and his effectiveness as a manager and facilitator of learning may, in some measure, depend on his command and deployment of technological aids to learning.

As yet, this teacher is uncommon but not altogether rare. Were it not for the demands—in energy, imagination, and time—that multidimensional teaching makes upon a teacher, the development of facilitators might proceed more rapidly than it has. I doubt that teachers will change sufficiently in these respects or that technological devices will become sufficiently automated to fulfill the promises about audio-visual instruction that still radiate from audio-visual (now instructional media) centers.

This argument is not meant to defend the teacher who never thinks past primitive modes of presentation. A teacher's voice, his gestures, his handling of text and chalk and blackboard can be developed in ways that make important differences between the mediocre classroom teacher and the expert one. The highly competent teacher is probably more receptive to technological aids than are his less competent colleagues. Using any aid to teaching takes more time and demands more commitment to teaching than does getting along without it. Central to the use of such aids is the teacher who can plan ahead, sense the best possibilities, work them into a design for having maximum impact on the students' learning.

The conclusion I draw is not that we must purchase more and more hardware, extend audio-visual services, require training in use of media. It is, rather, that we must increasingly respect the time, energy, imagination, and aptitude which can make the most of aids to teaching. Technology has had its impact. Probably it is too little employed. But if we are to secure its full use, we can do better by championing the exacting and exhausting craft of teaching rather than dwelling upon the prospects of technology. We get what we pay for in human beings as in machines. It must occur to many taxpayers that paying teachers year after year is more expensive than buying machines that keep grinding out lessons day after day. Still machines themselves have a limited life. Black and white gives way to color, the record player to the tape deck. In a close cost accounting, teachers, if they are spread thin enough, may still be the cheapest device for instruction. That, in part, may explain why so many teach in as economical a way as possible.

Third, classroom conditions for teaching vary from superb to mediocre to awful, with adequate but uninspiring probably descriptive of most. Midway in my visits to campuses, I was struck by how much the architecture reinforces the platform manner. Classrooms are not designed for conversation. For the most part, they are square or rectangular spaces in which varying numbers of people can be talked to or lectured at. In modern classrooms, the seats are movable, the blackboards green, and the erasers of an impossible sponge rubber construction inferior in every way to the old ones made of felt. Despite the wonders of indirect lighting and climate control, light, air, heat, and noise are often not under much better control than they were in the one-room schoolhouse. Teachers complain a good deal about classrooms, and the condition of classrooms should probably be counted among the sources of student dissatisfaction with teachers and teaching.

Auditoriums are probably least conducive to learning. The older ones are often in the grand style—the huge stage, the space between stage and seats, the seats stretching back into the dimness. For watching melodrama or operetta or mixed choruses, the arrangement is not bad. But for one man or woman addressing an audience and occasionally flicking a slide-projector button, it is awful. The numbers of students necessitate the continued use of such spaces, however inappropriate, on many campuses. Cheating, inattention, hostility, and cynicism on the part of students are probably more certain outcomes of such exposure than is learning of the subject matter.

Newer classrooms, deliberately designed for large numbers, are better. Blackboard space is doubled by two tiers of sliding

15

boards; space and basic equipment for demonstrations are provided (though I did not see much of it in use), and seating arrangements are designed to bring the students into closer contact with what goes on in front. A good deal of expertise has gone into designing new structures, and to an outside observer such attention seems to have justified itself.

In middle size classrooms, architectural ingenuity seems to have exhausted itself in variations on the size of rectangles, as the designer's skill is visible mainly in the shape of and materials used in the chairs. Even these accomplishments are not to be shrugged aside, for color and comfort make a difference in a classroom and are not particularly expensive to provide. (Hooks upon which to hang coats, for example, are not expensive, but they are too rarely in evidence.) The rectangle itself can be employed wisely or unwisely. It is not, for example, profitable to stretch the rectangle too far. A room much more than twice as long as it is wide defeats instruction at the outset. The teacher exhausts himself (microphone or not) peering down a tube or, switching arrangements, trying to look right and left like a mid-court spectator at a tennis match.

Small rooms are small rooms. Most official classrooms lack style, ease, and grace, though some affluent departments manage special seminar rooms not unlike those enjoyed by affluent business concerns. Few of either kind have more than chairs around a table to distinguish their function.

I do not wonder at student pressure for living-learning centers and chronic pleas to get out of the classrooms for some class meetings. Perhaps the best that can be said of classrooms (and this may be part of the theory of their design) is that they enhance learning by making other spaces, where students do spend most of their time, that much more attractive. Western campuses, particularly, have made much use of open space outside as a part of the building plan itself. And fairly often in new buildings I saw evidence of intelligent attention to the relation between design and learning. In many instances, limitations on space and funds and an architectural design imposed by the past present inescapable problems. Even so, to my mind the interior space of classrooms has received the least attention in new buildings and old.

Professors in the Classroom

Classes in their variety and number do not fit available space which is even reasonably appropriate and therefore spill out to wherever they can be taught. No one should pick on an individual campus space coordinator or room assigner. He works from charts and boxes and sees the classrooms as he gets complaints from those who are assigned them. In time, he gets to know most classrooms fairly well, thereby ruining himself for the job; intimate acquaintance with available spaces makes it impossible for him to put anyone in some of them.

Students and, to a lesser degree, faculty have always subverted the designs of management. A member of the English department at Western Michigan University told me that 20 per cent of the English classes there were being held off campus. No one had planned it; students and teachers had apparently just drifted off to what were regarded as congenial surroundings. Traditionally, such privileges as meeting in a faculty member's home or a tavern or a coffee house have been reserved for the graduate seminar or for such unacademic pursuits as creative writing. But here, apparently, was a movement of another kind, temporary perhaps until some member of the administration became worried or students tired of sitting on the floor, but a useful escape from the four classroom walls. At the same university, I heard of a war of attrition between students and a building custodian. The students moved the chairs out of a given classroom and installed their own pillows, pads, and prayer rugs. The custodian moved the chairs back in, the students brought back their own furnishings. Eventually, the administration had to take a hand. I do not know whether the room was sealed off, the custodian was transferred, or the students were made to get off the floor and sit up like ladies and gentlemen. The incident is probably only one among hundreds in which the current generation has resisted generally unattractive classroom space.

Good teachers can rise above their physical surroundings, as they can rise above both their colleagues and their students. But it is not well to assume always and in all three of these particulars that rising above is the best alternative. "It is not the size of the class that matters," one professor passed on to me, "but the size of the man who's up in front." Undoubtedly, in an inexact way, such

17

utterances enshrine truth. But they do not add much to the knowledge that might help settle the arguments about big and small classes and that might make for good management of class size. Similarly, the teacher is more important to what happens in the classroom than is the classroom itself. But classrooms have their importance, and their basic designs and the uses made of them are often opposed to the teaching and learning which is supposed to be taking place.

Fourth, what is taught and how it is taught (apart from the individual teacher) go on in one place much as they go on in another. It continues to depress me, even as I teach my own courses, to think of the thousands all over the country doing much the same thing in the same kinds of places at the same hour. It is also in the nature of mass education (of life, for that matter) that it be so. But these visions aside, the sameness of curriculum and credit hours and assignments and testing and grading and certifying is not very inspiring to one who thinks about the variety of individuals subjected to the process.

When one considers the many courses found within a college or university catalog and the freedom of choice which has increasingly been permitted, he may doubt the validity of this observation. Yet, the number of courses is not a measure of variety. A course in the history of early Islamic culture taught by the lecture method to one hundred students in a classroom in Michigan is not very different from a course in the principles of marketing taught by the same method to the same numbers in Arizona. Similarly, choice of titles of classes means little if the basic framework—method, class hours, credit, grading—is the same.

Such considerations may help explain why the proliferation of courses, which the administrator blames on the faculty, goes on and why students demand even more courses from the faculty. How is it possible that in universities which already have 2000 courses, students set up free universities to supply 2000-plus? It is not only that each student, like each professor, wants his or her courses. It is also that the sameness of courses, whatever their apparent number, strikingly reduces the alternatives. The lecture method persists because it is one of the few ways we have—however we modify the specific means of delivery—of communicating information in a person-to-person way. Numbers of courses may increase without adding variety to the curriculum.

What is to be done? The best chance of reducing the number of courses while increasing the variety is to let a spirit of ad hocness enter the curriculum. A number of admittedly imperfect studies confirm what common sense has already declared: any new course gets better the first few times it is taught but probably gets worse year by year thereafter. Professors who teach the same course from the same yellowed notes to generations of students do exist. The nature both of the collegiate structure and of the teachers within it inclines to the preservation and addition of courses rather than to any rhythmic creation and destruction. The best improvement in any curriculum may follow from a firm agreement that no course last beyond five years. It may not even matter too much if faculty members subvert the intent by seeing to it that many changes are in name only. Even that mild rearrangement is missing in the present system, by which classes once admitted to the catalog tend to stay forever.

Some specific arrangements for getting around fixed course practices have been developed in the past few years. Blackboard courses are a way of satisfying temporary student interests without setting up off-campus enterprises or complicating the internal machinery. Under such an arrangement, students within a department or a college can write on a blackboard a course they would like to have. If enough other students add their names, the department tries to find a teacher, and the class comes into being. A consequential means of varying class offerings as well as methodology is the interim term arrangement. At Coe College, for example, the calendar is now on a 4-1-4 basis, with the middle semester being a January exploratory term. During this period, faculty members can offer different courses, conduct them in quite different ways, and meet both their own and the students' need to break away from the sameness of formal routines. A term which offered, as Coe did in 1970, a course taught by a mathematician described as "an investigation of the life (such as it was)' and the writings (no parenthetical apology necessary) of Jane Austen"; one on Charlie Chap-

19

lin, Duke Ellington, William Faulkner, and Jean Dubuffet; and one called The Many Facets of Dishonesty had a good deal going for it. How much the term achieves over a long span probably depends on the willingness of the faculty to keep it exploratory even to the point of getting rid of it entirely when it no longer offers the best means of exploration.

It is an encouraging sign that grades, which are a central part of the countinghouse philosophy which enforces conformity, are everywhere under examination. It is a backward school right now which does not have some alternatives to the A-E grading system. So extensive has been the movement to pass-fail or credit—no-credit alternatives that Phi Beta Kappa is examining its traditional practice of basing election to the society largely on grade-point averages. Together with some movement toward increased use of proficiency examinations for course credit, eventually to the external degree, and perhaps to the three-year bachelor's degree as the Carnegie Commission has advocated, the loosening up of academic practices may portend a general lifting of the constraints that courses, credit hours, grades, and degree certification have placed upon teaching.

CHAPTER 2

Attitudes
Toward Teaching

The following observations also grew out of campus visits, but were shaped more by talks with members of the academic community than by classroom observations. The appearances I made before general campus audiences were always open ended. I received a good many unsolicited opinions as well as responses shaped by the nature of my remarks. Since there never were many students in attendance at the open meetings, I made a deliberate attempt to talk to student groups. Sometimes I spoke to those who were involved in student government; fairly often I struck up conversations with students wherever I found the opportunity. I did not let these casual acquaintances know at the start of my connection with a project to improve teaching, nor did I invite them to be critical of their professors. I expressed the curiosity I thought might be natural to any middle-aged visitor wondering what kind of educational experience the students were having. The students took it from there. I had a number of extended conversations with student and faculty groups about some of the specific observations I was making. At the University of North Carolina at Greensboro, for example, a

21

group of students told me a great deal about just what students meant when they criticized professors "who didn't care." It was one of the most enlightening evenings in my travels and important to me, for that complaint was voiced by students everywhere. The gist of our discussion that evening relates to the first of my observations about student and faculty attitudes: Students are extremely critical of undergraduate teachers and teaching.

In all the groups I talked to on many campuses, instances of bad teaching came out much more quickly than instances of good teaching. Perhaps evil always has a higher visibility than good or perhaps really bad teachers cast a shadow over all other experience. Whatever the reasons, the negative effects of teaching seem to be more at the front of student recall than are the positive aspects. Moreover, wherever I went, there seemed to be a remarkable similarity in the students' complaints about teachers as well as in their praise.

Students were most put off by teachers who did not care or who didn't seem to care. *Caring* is a word, like *relevance,* which has been so frequently used by students that it has aroused distrust among faculty members. But I have had little reason to distrust the validity of the students' reactions when I have had the chance to pin them down about what they meant by caring. Clearly, their reactions were a good deal less sentimental and personal than many faculty members think. They did not hearken back to any Mr. Chips past, real or imagined. The students I spoke with seemed as sensitive as faculty to the need for maintaining some sense of difference between students and faculty. They did not want an arm over the shoulder, a let's-all-rap-about-it-in-someone's-pad kind of familiarity. What they wanted was a teacher able to convey a sense of caring about what he was doing and somehow to make that concern include both the students and the world outside the campus.

The need for caring seemed to be as intense on small campuses as it was on large ones. It reminded me of the spring quarter in 1967, which I spent as a visiting professor at Carleton College. The atmosphere in this small, somewhat remote but prestigious liberal arts college is informal, and as a visitor I probably had more opportunity to sound out student attitudes than the regular staff did. It puzzled me that almost the first student comments I heard were complaints that the faculty was too distant. "What do you want?" I said at the time. "If you were any closer you'd be living with them." Northfield is a small town and the faculty houses are close to the campus. When winter comes down in Minnesota, there is no escaping one another until spring. But by the end of that quarter, I had a feeling the students were right. The faculty members were fairly distant. They were even fairly distant from me and I from them. We had our individual ponderings to do, and I have since met Carleton faculty members who were on the campus that spring and who were surprised to find that I was there during the same period.

Students are locked into departments early, and faculty members' allegiance to subject matter and discipline is about as fierce within highly regarded liberal arts colleges as anywhere. Each faculty member cares about his place in his scholarly discipline, his immediate chances for advancement if he is young or completion of lifelong plans if he is old, and his private life away from the classroom. The very nature of higher education creates barriers between students and professors. These barriers stem not only from the pomposity to which academic rank and afflictions of intellect may incline professors. They also come from an honest respect for the objectivity of scholarship, from the necessity to keep personal and subjective elements from contaminating truth. The useful distances which forms of address, classroom routines, formal office hours, and the like maintain are widened by the necessity for maintaining scholarly detachment. Urgings on the part of youth "to let it all hang out" do not reach a generation of professors schooled in the measured, judicious, thoroughly examined response to any phenomenon. We are dealing with old attitudes which create distance between students and professors, attitudes probably exaggerated by the current stances of a vigorous and often irritating youth culture.

So distances are created both from professors' not caring and from their difficulties in making students aware that they do care. Students are harshest on professors who, they claim, do not care about anything they are doing. Teaching is a drag, the students an annoyance, the institution a caricature of a civilized intellectual community. Or, teaching is a routine which obviously exacts less from the professor than he gives to other interests. The current surplus of Ph.D.s only underlines an obvious fact of academic placement: the number of professors trained in eminent places for lofty pursuits far exceeds the number who can find such places to teach in. Such displacements breed a disdain to which students are rightly sensitive, and the general improvement of teaching might profitably start with an attempt to change faculty attitudes toward their positions and their institutions.

The quality students praise most often in teachers is almost the exact opposite of what they criticize. In today's parlance, they want someone who turns them on. Perhaps the metaphor is not completely descriptive, for it fails to suggest the diverse ways students get turned on. Call it impact, impression, or what you will. It cannot be achieved without some personal dimensions, and yet it does not necessarily mean charisma or glitter or brilliance or overwhelming charm. The diversity of students makes it possible for many teachers to be extraordinary teachers on their own terms. There does not seem to be one style, one single standard of discipline or of intellect, any specific degree of vigor or openness that must be attained if a teacher is to turn others on. The instructor needs style and standards and vigor and openness—generosity, above all—but these can be developed by any professor in accordance with his own personality and character.

I have also observed that faculty members respect teaching and are somewhat interested in it, but comparatively few incline toward developing teaching as an art or themselves primarily as teachers. I hasten to explain what may strike the reader as a curiously indefinite way of describing the interest of college teachers in teaching. The phrasing is vague, but deliberately so, even precisely so. Throughout my travels, I did not hear faculty members express disrespect for teaching. Keep in mind that on the campuses I visited, even those which vigorously spread word of my coming and of my mission—to improve college teaching—I seldom encountered a majority of the faculty. Teaching is not a subject to attract large numbers of faculty on a college or university campus. Such a commonplace and general topic promises too few rewards to draw fac-

ulty members away from other concerns. But despite these reservations about the number of faculty members who are likely to give
attention to teaching, I can honestly say I was well received on all
campuses, perhaps better than might be expected for a stranger
coming around to improve something.

The most accurate term I can find for the common faculty
attitude is *respect*. It is not *enthusiasm,* though enthusiasm can be
aroused among many faculty members once discussion gets going
about the particulars of teaching. It is not *hostility*. Although many
faculty members get impatient with teaching and many find ways
of reducing the burden, few are hostile toward it. And, finally, the
most common attitude is not *interest,* at least not for the majority
of faculty at any given time.

I say *somewhat interested* to describe the attitude which I
think generally prevails and which is in part measured by the presence or absence of active signs of interest: attending the discussions
I held or others like them, taking part in group activities aimed at
teaching, consciously working at teaching on one's own. Interest is
not very high whether measured by the presence of these signs or
by the intensity of sustained interest which gives teaching priority
over all other faculty responsibilities. But, by either measure, interest is not lacking on any campus. It is my guess that interest has
risen in the last few years and will continue to rise.

Finally, I see comparatively few—fewer than half the faculty
on even small campuses supposedly devoted to teaching, and many
fewer than half in large universities—who incline toward developing teaching as an art. Some individuals prefer to call teaching a
craft rather than art, just as some want to consider it a science. I
have no objection to regarding teaching as an art or a craft, though
I have some strong objections to regarding it as a science. But few
college teachers give sufficient attention to teaching itself to see its
full dimensions as a craft, an art, or even a science. What dazzles
me about teaching is the expanding opportunity it affords for development. And what depresses me is how, for so many teachers I
encounter, this endless variety seems to be lost in the routines of presentation, the sameness of students, the vexations of preparations
that get in the way of other important matters. I do not know how

to get around the attitudes which stand in the way of getting more faculty members—by no means all or even all the time—to commit themselves to teaching as they commit themselves to writing poetry or music or to performing on a stage or to pursuing a line of scholarly investigation. When I face these attitudes, I am inclined to give up and agree with those who say teachers, like artists if not craftsmen, are born, not made. And yet, of teachers and artists, this statement is less than a half-truth. We learn to teach. If we learn to teach with a very high degree of skill, we do so because we regard it as craft or art worthy of our acquiring the powers, the techniques, and the sensitivity to do it extremely well.

In the course of my visits, the way to improve teaching most frequently suggested by the faculty members I met was to change the reward system. This subject I also discuss at length in a later chapter. I think there are good arguments for this position. Some abuses offer obvious targets for reform. Other aspects of the reward system, however, are complex matters as they affect teaching. We must carefully consider the ways of bringing about change as well as the effects of change.

In most institutions, the goals of the institution, the expectations communicated to individual faculty members, and the criteria for determining how or whether these expectations have been met need to be precisely defined and frequently and openly examined, revised, and restated. Unless this is done, the general expectations of achievements in research, teaching, and service are held up for everyone and judged imprecisely for everyone. The most widely voiced criticism of the reward system is that teaching is pitted against research and therefore teaching is neglected because research results are more visible and more related to desired accomplishments within department and discipline. Arguments which pit teaching against service are not as often voiced probably because teaching is often regarded as a form of service. In institutions where teaching is primary, service may be a more important means of fulfilling faculty responsibilities than is research.

Nevertheless in all institutions, including community colleges, advanced scholarly work, whether it is connected with actual research or not, is usually rewarded. (In the public schools, the

M.A., Ph.D., or equivalent hours of graduate work are commonly related to steps in the salary scale.) It is assumed that continued schooling means better teaching. This is one of the assumptions which adds complexity to any consideration of the reward system. Within that segment of the higher education system where the Ph.D. is regarded as a minimum requirement for a position, this assumption is tempered by another assumption—that the primary mission of higher education is the discovery of knowledge, call it research, and that the Ph.D. is evidence of a minimum degree of research competence.

Jessie Bernard makes a distinction between the role of *teacher* and that of *man-of-knowledge*.[1] (It is worth noting that the phrase is not *woman-of-knowledge*. Women in the university are generally associated with the lower forms of teaching, those furthest removed from the functions of the man-of-knowledge.) "The role of teacher," she writes, "is to serve as an instrument of communication; the role of the man-of-knowledge is to serve as a collaborator with the original author."[2] She points out other distinctions: the teacher deals with the established, hence usually elementary, aspects of his discipline, the man-of-knowledge deals with the "controversial, hence usually with advanced, aspects"; the teacher, to a certain extent, must coerce students to learn, the man-of-knowledge invites students to share enthusiasm for the subject matter with him; the teacher socializes the student into his citizenship role, the man-of-knowledge into his intellectual role.

It is disconcerting that the author seems to accept these distinctions as somehow validated by the order of the universe rather than seeing them as expressions of values held by the university. The distinction can be found in title and somewhat in practice in the designation of public school personnel as teachers and university faculty as professors. But within higher education, we must go back to the early years of Vassar and Smith to find women faculty members designated teachers and males, professors. In present prac-

---

[1] *Academic Women* (University Park, Pa.: Pennsylvania State University Press, 1964), pp. 115–119.
[2] *Ibid.,* p. 116.

tice, admittedly, some men and many women are consigned to the role of teacher even though they may carry, for a lifetime, the title assistant professor. Such practices seem to me to be evidences of the dubious values upon which the reward system rests. The heart of the system is a belief that teaching is inferior to working with, contributing to, and pursuing knowledge.

The larger arguments are taken up in a later chapter. I am not convinced that the pursuing of knowledge as I see it carried out by a cross-section of college and university faculties is of any higher worth than the teaching they do. Excellence in university teaching, it seems to me, makes scholarly demands fully as great as the pursuit of knowledge, though the nature of the demands may be somewhat different. By ability, temperament, and inclination, some faculty members give priority to one or the other, but this preference is usually a matter of degree rather than of exclusion. The valid distinction may concern what a person can do at a given time. A minimum reward system should lead faculty members to pursue knowledge and to profess it, to devote their energies to one at some periods and to the other at other times. The system should give all members of the faculty the opportunity and incentive to develop both as teachers and as men-and-women-of-knowledge.

Research vs. teaching is the central issue in disputes about the reward system. Empirical studies using various measures of teaching effectiveness and of research ability and productivity have not produced clear evidence of a relationship between a faculty member's research activities and the quality of his teaching. The studies themselves are little more convincing than faculty debates. Some excellent researchers are excellent teachers; some are not. Some excellent teachers do not publish much; some do. In the end, institutions probably act on assumptions not unlike those which assume that continued schooling means better teaching and that the primary mission of higher education is the discovery of knowledge. Because of these assumptions as well as because of changes in institutional goals, the constant reexamining of the reward system within individual institutions is vital to making the system more favorable to teaching. Such reexaminations should result in frequent updating of the values of the institution and frequent revision of written statements setting forth specific criteria and procedures for advancement.

Without strenuous attempts to make our values clear and current, we flounder among general arguments about institutional aims and individual worth based more on personal preference and prejudice than on judgment. Research cannot simply be put aside and the energies and intelligence thus released channeled into superior teaching. But the pressure to publish is real, and publications weigh heavily in considerations for promotion. Service is seldom defined precisely in university promotion structures, just as the quality of research is often as inaccurately weighed as the effectiveness of teaching. There are some signs—the interest and acceptance of student evaluation of teaching, for example—that the reward system is being examined. This structure needs examination not only now but steadily since it is such a strong motivating force within individual institutions and within the profession.

My experience with this subject has convinced me that what makes an effective or ineffective teacher in the classroom can be identified, profitably discussed, and fairly evaluated. Beyond their use in evaluation, our knowledge and experience of teaching effectiveness could be used much more effectively to develop teachers than they are now, particularly in graduate schools. This subject is discussed more fully in *The Recognition and Evaluation of Teaching*.[3] The response to that booklet has been greater than sponsoring groups expected. Evaluation of teachers by students, a major theme in the booklet, is by now probably accepted by a majority of faculty members. The strong possibility that these evaluations will be used in decisions on retention, promotion, and tenure adds to the impact they may have on the improvement of teaching.

Since the booklet was published, two considerations have arisen which were not stressed there. One is that student interest in evaluating faculty may wane. If faculty members find student evaluation useful in improving individual competence and in providing supporting data for decisions on advancement, the faculty itself may have to actively seek the students' cooperation. I think cooperation will be forthcoming if sought, and students may welcome the as-

[3] K. Eble (Washington, D.C.: American Association of University Professors and Association of American Colleges, 1970).

sistance faculty and administrators can give. Getting students and faculty to think about qualities that contribute to effective teaching is a means of improving the learning environment for both.

The other consideration is that the search for an exact and comprehensive means of evaluating teaching should not stand in the way of using the means we possess. Faculty members, in general, are not well informed about research on various aspects of evaluating teaching. Though such research, like much of the research in human behavior, is limited in its exactness and what it can prove, results are reasonably consistent from one study to another. If faculty members kept in mind that student evaluations provide feedback principally on one aspect of effective teaching—classroom performance—they would have less reason to question their validity or be suspicious of their use.

Student evaluation has revealed to a wide range of faculty members the investigations that have been made of classroom performance. Student feedback has opened up for discussion qualities of the effective teacher that have been accepted as working principles but somewhat resisted as trustworthy information. Evaluation has also caused members of the academic community to consider whether, in fact, the specifics of effective teaching can be identified with sufficient accuracy to play a large part in judgments of faculty competence. These are all important considerations in the continuing search for further understanding of teaching and learning. The subject is of such great importance that it should be studied, if not formally researched, by everyone engaged in teaching. Amid the imperfect means now being used to judge a professor's competence, responsible judgments of teaching seem to offer more exact data than do other parts of the process. Student ratings, visitation of classes, critiques of audio or video tape, team teaching, and self-analysis are all means by which the outward, immediate acts of teaching can be examined. The more difficult task of trying to measure what students learn and to relate it to how that learning came about brings us to another dimension of the process of examining teaching which is discussed at length in Chapter Four.

Evaluation of individual performance may not, in the long

run, be the chief purpose of such inquiries. Wider understanding of teaching and learning processes may be the more important consequence. We have already learned enough to incorporate our knowledge into the graduate programs of prospective college teachers. In fact, graduate faculties possess the experience and practical knowledge that should become integral parts of the limited experience graduate students get as teachers. Recognition of the importance of teaching is crucial to such a development and ultimately may be more important than evaluation.

Another observation: Teachers today face a great deal of competition. Some of it is peculiar to the present age, but much of this competition probably confronted teachers in previous times. Many teachers are seriously bothered by the superior power of television, radio, and film to shape their students and by the influence of a nervous and mindless culture. How can learning, and the demands it makes on the exercise of intellect, go on at all when the culture continually floods the young with immediate sensory satisfactions? No teacher can escape trying to find working answers to this question.

Some attitudes, however, stand in the way of even seeking answers. One such attitude is a suspicion of learning as pleasure, of popularity as a measure of good teaching. If it does not hurt, this attitude assumes, it cannot be doing good. If it is not faintly boring, it cannot be educational. I will not review the debate in the substantial literature on human learning over whether reward or punishment, anticipation of pleasure or fear of pain, is the most important incitement to learning. Modern theory which inclines to favor pleasure and reward may be merely a product of a hedonistic age. Students learn from teachers and experiences they hate and fear. They also learn from those they love, and love has more chance of enlarging the human spirit than does hate or fear.

Aside from these larger arguments, I often encountered a distrust of the popular teacher which makes some faculty members seem unduly misanthropic. Without challenging anecdotal information about mean or dull or arrogant professors who turned out to be the teachers from whom some people learned most, I would still

31

counsel teachers to lean toward using the pleasure of learning or, at least, not to deliberately oppose these pleasures.

Part of the competition every teacher faces is the resistance of students. The enemy is not television or the seductive arguments of advertising or even the superior pleasures our culture generously affords. The enemy is human nature or at least those parts of human nature which resist discipline, knowledge, and thought. This resistance has not arisen with the advent of the light bulb or the automobile. If we start with written records, which are a product of discipline, rationality, and thought, we find that most human beings have always lived pretty close to their skins. The teacher has always worked against the competition of circuses and song, fair skies and the open road. I think it is worthwhile to examine the impact of our culture and to use that knowledge in teaching, but to think that our peculiar age has overpowered the teacher is a narrow, time-bound view, as limited to the perspective of the present as are the attitudes of students supposedly ruined by modern life.

In watching teachers and students as an outside observer, I was interested to see how unmindful many teachers were of competition. One small way in which good teachers may differ from poor ones is the sensitivity they have and express to matters outside the classroom. Given the assassination of a towering figure like John F. Kennedy, for example, few teachers could proceed as usual. That tragedy was acknowledged in classrooms, as it should have been, in response to the need for all of us to share the common woe. But given lesser events, the passing of some less stately figure, routine newspaper headlines, the changes of season, most professors proceed at chapter three, paragraph, two, page twenty-one, just where they left off the previous hour. Gilbert Highet, a superb lecturer at Columbia, began most of his lectures with some reference to something he had seen on the way to class or a story currently getting newspaper attention or an observation about a current book he was reading or an activity he had been enjoying. Sometimes he shaped these observations to fit the current class topic. An oil tanker scandal could put him in mind of what Juvenal had to say about Roman embezzlers. But often the references served the dual purpose of letting students settle down in their seats and of acknowledging that

32

we had all come to class from the world outside and would be returning before long.

Students are still surprised when they learn professors dance or drink or play baseball—not specific professors, perhaps, but professors in general. Even today, when some professors try to stay out in front of the students (and as often turn students off as turn them on), the majority still act in the classroom in ways designed to arouse surprise when students catch them acting like human beings outside. This is a healthy condition, and I would regret the disappearance of such surprises by which we move from generalization about types to recognition of individuals. Still, I think it would be well for professors not to leave their humanity outside the classroom door.

I have no idea whether we are in a bad age or a good one for formal higher learning. The means we possess certainly suggest a good age; the distractions which seem to be everywhere may make it seem bad. Compared with the professor's lot in any past age, in most material respects, his situation now is not bad, no matter where any individual professor places himself on the scales of social respect, material well-being, or personal satisfactions.

Teaching is always a competitive activity. Every time we enter a classroom or have a student enter an office or sit quietly plotting what we are going to do the next hour, we must think in terms of what other things are demanding attention. For the most part, we do it unconsciously by furnishing a comfortable chair or lowering the blinds to keep the sun out of a visitor's eyes or helping a student find a place for an armful of books. Sometimes we probe (sensitively I hope) into what may be bothering the student. Other times, we trim our demands or stretch our deadlines. Whatever we do, we probably do it better in one-to-one confrontations. Given a classroom full of students, it is easy to resolve all the individuals into something called the class, the class hour into as inviolate a concept as the classroom and from then on fail to acknowledge any competition. Some teachers have such magnificent presence that they can shut off the outside world. But speaking of the general run of teachers, I wish they were more mindful of the competition they face, more honest and open and generous with themselves and

their students about the presence of competition, and more inge-
nious and energetic in meeting it.

I put down my last observation just as it appeared as the
tenth item in a list which attempted to summarize the results of my
classroom visits: Certain attitudes on the part of teachers and students, I wrote, seem to evidence themselves to me as I visited and
talked to individuals and groups. I read this list, including the concluding item, during a discussion with recipients of Danforth graduate fellowships for women. They wanted to hear my observations
about teaching, and I had not yet filled out all the items in the
list—or even looked back at my notes for several months. As I began
reading the last observation, I became aware that I had no idea
of what it meant. As I admitted to them, it must have meant something when I wrote it down. I like to think that if I could just
figure out what it was, I would have the whole key to the mysteries
of teaching and the ways of improving it.

I put the sentence down here for its cautionary effect. Teaching proceeds so much by rhetoric that teachers must be forcefully
and often jarred into recognizing how much rhetoric betrays us.
Every undergraduate class has someone who can mimic the manner, the phrasings, the pauses, and the pet words and gestures of
any number of professors. In itself, that may not say too much
about a teacher's effectiveness. But to the extent such a characteriza-
tion dwells on the professor's reliance on patterns, his repetition of
phrases, the stockness of his responses, it says important and unfavorable things about that professor's teaching style.

One is never quite sure whether there are three important
points because there really are three or because rhetoric has us saying, "The three (or five or eight or fifteen) most important characteristics are . . ." One does not know whether it really is "on
the one hand" or "on the other" or whether the convenience of language makes it seem so. One is never sure whether "perhaps" pref-
aces an outright lie or a bare possibility, or whether it just indicates
unwillingness to be pinned down. Our language is such that given a
platform, an audience, and some years at putting sentences together,
one can put down a sentence like my "final observation" with every
honest intention of being both clear and profound.

34

Attitudes Toward Teaching

I leave the sentence as it stands for it shows my own uneasiness that I had only nine observations to make and was straining for a tenth because ten might signify a more comprehensive view. There may, after all, have been only four points, or seven, or twenty-five.

CHAPTER 3

Teaching Effectively

D espite the vast collective experience teachers can draw upon, there are still genuine questions as to whether teaching can be reduced to any set of essentials. The individuality of the teacher and of the students, the particular characteristics of subject matter, the multiple goals of learning, the contexts of teaching and learning—all seem to defy any clear statement about how a good teacher should go about the task. Wilbert McKeachie's *Teaching Tips* is a good, practical handbook for the beginning college teacher; Gilbert Highet's *The Art of Teaching* is also a very valuable book; and Whitehead's *Aims of Education* should be read every year. There are a great many others, but all fall somewhat short of the realities of working with students and the mysteries of how or whether the teacher's work is actually furthering student learning.

The subject is discussed at length in *The Recognition and Evaluation of Teaching*.[1] Evaluation must rest upon knowledge of what good teaching is. The booklet advances this line of reasoning:

[1] Eble, pp. 1–20.

Teaching Effectively

We know a good deal about effective and ineffective teaching. Certainly the hundreds of thousands of teachers who appear before students every day have some sense of the effectiveness or ineffectiveness of what they are doing. The individual teacher knows, in the pragmatic sense, that this direction is better than another, this approach has worked in the past and may work today, that these acts and attitudes on his part seem to invite the student in and incline him, at the least, toward learning. It is Socratic wisdom that the mark of the knowing teacher is that he *knows* very little. Of the teaching process itself, he may only *know* that he must be constantly ready to drop old strategies and adopt new ones. But this *knowing* is part of the essential wisdom of any man or woman on the way to becoming educated: that few things are certain, that time and events require a continuing effort to recast what is known and to seek new ways of knowing as well as new knowledge itself.[2]

The discussion of effective teaching in the booklet is limited because of the necessity of focusing on ways, means, and uses of evaluation. Both beginning and experienced teachers have shown great interest in what constitutes effective teaching, implying that the project should sort out basic principles and publish them along with its other findings. The following observations about teaching are not presented as being definitive, startling, or new. They are set down chiefly because of my beliefs that the craft of teaching can be developed and that the academic profession has the fundamental responsibility for the development of that craft.

First, in teaching as in writing, a person can go wrong in all the right directions. There must be discipline in teaching, but discipline goes over into rigidity as easily as informality becomes sloppiness. Examples and illustrations are vital but they may lead teachers and students into endless digressions. Specification is essential but a teacher can lose his students in a forest of detail. There is nothing to be alarmed about in these observations. All crafts and arts proceed to some degree by testing directions, pushing on when things work out favorably, and pulling back when they do not. Two other major cautions need emphasis. First, students vary, classes vary, teachers vary, class by class, hour by hour. Nothing works

[2] *Ibid.*, pp. 8–9.

every time. A student told me of a professor who had pasted a sign on his office door: "NEVER HAVE TWO BAD ONES IN A ROW." The second caution is that no teacher knows exactly how much learning is taking place. If he is skillful and conscientious, he has rough measures—tests, conferences, student work—and he can hardly succeed as a performer without an immediate sense of what is getting across. Still, humility about what is being accomplished and continuing efforts to find out are proper responses. Having stated these cautions, I think they are no cause for more than the ordinary despair. Endless possibilities are the chief attractions of teaching. Within those possibilities, good teachers develop their craft. The skilled craftsman, it must be assumed, has a better chance of effecting learning than one who is not.

Second, generosity is surely an essential of good teaching. I might not consider it so important tomorrow, nor would I have included it in any list of essentials when I began teaching, but my campus observations have brought it regularly to mind. Why is generosity so vital? Because, if we feel that teaching and teachers need improvement, generosity could probably do more than anything else. The flight from teaching, as a Carnegie report once described it, was far from an involuntary exodus though there are chronic shortcomings in the support of teachers that force many people away. In the colleges and universities, this exodus took place chiefly because large numbers of academically trained individuals had their eyes on the main chance. With an abundance of scholarly and teaching talent in the sixties, only a want of generosity explains the relatively weak commitment to teaching during that decade. Individual teachers must have some generosity of spirit or they will not remain satisfyingly attached to their profession. I do not refer simply to the economic position of the teacher—still unfavorable as compared with other professions—but to the fact that teaching demands a great deal of giving. Giving of self—personality and character—as well as of energy, time, skill, and knowledge are required. It is philosophically possible to regard such giving as a means of fulfillment, but that is a hard attitude to adopt and a harder one to practice day by day.

But generosity in this larger sense is not really what I mean.

Generosity of outlook, translated into daily practice, is closer to teaching itself. Generosity in outlook means resisting the tendency to regard knowledge and the institution's packaging and certifying of it as things which must be husbanded away. We all recognize that a commodity may be cheapened if it becomes widely available, that people may not value that which comes too easily. But indiscriminate giving would alter the meaning of generosity, and higher education is a long way from making its products too easy to obtain. Individual teachers should seek occasions to be generous, to use generosity in providing motivation.

A wise teacher of physics, Julius Taylor, told me that his most successful teaching practice was every so often to "let them win one." Physics can be a tough course; the exactness of fundamental mathematics forces testing into a framework of absolute right or wrong, and grades can be rough as a consequence. What Professor Taylor did was periodically to construct a test which even the laggards could pass (to be generous, you may have to risk being charitable toward willful laziness as well as toward unavoidable slowness of mind). Giving the student a chance to succeed, Professor Taylor reasoned, might lead to more success. A constantly failing student is likely to expect failure.

Teachers forget, even while current students noisily remind them, that they exercise great power over the students. The final grade is a mortgage which can easily be foreclosed at the last moment of a term. If grades are to regain even marginal utility for motivation and evaluation, they will probably have to become infused with a spirit of generosity. The fact that grades have been modified, that pass/fail and credit/no credit marks are common, may in part be explained by some growth in faculty generosity. Intermixed as it is with student pressure and faculty impatience, the increase in generosity may not be large. Nevertheless, a faculty's generosity, or lack of it, is often exposed in debates over grades. Yielding on one front is usually followed by regrouping on another. ABCDE in time give way to High Pass, Pass, Low Pass, Fail. Or pass/fail grades are permitted except—and the list of exceptions is often long. One may question why we give failing grades at all. Students pay whether they fail or pass and it appears grasping and punitive to collect tuition, withhold credit, and brand the person through his permanent record. We would give up little if we abandoned the punitive aspects of grading. We would give little away if we found ways of shaping and giving assignments which increased our chances of being able to praise students. We would not do irreparable harm to the bell-shaped curve if we found ways to put larger numbers on the high side. And we would have most learning theory on our side if we acted in ways designed to keep learning pleasurable for a maximum number of students.

There is another kind of generosity we must exhibit if learning is to go well. We must fight off the feeling that particular students or institutions are not worthy of our effort. There are bad students, I suppose, and bad institutions, I know, but there are also bad teachers, including those who stay with bad students in bad places because they have neither the courage to leave nor the fortitude to fight for better conditions nor the practical wisdom to do what they can. Teachers can, if they choose, shift responsibility for good teaching to the school or to classroom conditions or to the abilities, interests, backgrounds, etc., etc., etc. of the students. It would be better to follow Whitehead's advice: "It should be the chief aim of the university professor to exhibit himself in his own true character—that is, as an ignorant man thinking."[3] Why should students not be ignorant? What is fulfilling about teaching students who are already brighter than we are?

I say these things with sharpness, but not without acknowledging that conditions may be deplorable in some places. I am not so sure that students are deplorable anywhere. Good teachers oftentimes manage to develop some possibilities in students other teachers have given up as hopeless. Resignation to things as they are, acquiescence to bad conditions, should not be confused with generosity. Good teaching is neither resigned nor acquiescent. In fact, it may be the generous teachers who give their time to changing conditions that jar a school, its students and teachers, out of their hopelessness. The really effective teacher must exert himself for the students he has wherever he is and be generous enough to risk wast-

[3] A. N. Whitehead, *The Aims of Education* (New York: Mentor Books, 1949), p. 48.

ing all his efforts. If his efforts seem to come to nothing or if the returns are too small to justify the expenditure of psychic energy, it is better to try another place or another occupation than to risk permanent meanness of spirit.

Third, energy is often an outstanding characteristic of the effective teacher. Like generosity, energy is often overlooked. As I watched many classes and reflected upon those where something seemed to be happening in the learning space between teacher and student, I often concluded that the teacher's energy made the difference. Teachers are aware of the energy required when they come away drained from an effective class. Students ought, perhaps, to be grateful for the scarcity of teachers operating at high energy levels; continuing exposure from class to class would be too exhausting.

Physical energy is part of what is needed. Young teachers, insecure for various reasons with familiar classroom impedimenta to hide behind, sometimes refrain from fully drawing upon their physical resources. The college teacher no longer has to whip the biggest boy in the class to establish his authority, but he may have to exhibit superior physical and mental energy in order to induce the students to invest more of theirs. Teachers probably pick up the physical tricks of teaching in proportion to their histrionic talent or their lack of inhibitions. But by leaving such important developments to inclination alone, we fail to recognize that there are a number of principles and a range of practices which can be taught. Movement, for example, is important. Effective teachers move toward their students as they ask questions. A moving object catches more attention than a static one. Gestures are immensely meaningful for the actor and for all of us in our daily exchanges with other people. Even the voice has physical dimensions.

Reviewing voice and gesture control, which are commonplace to those in the performing arts, is less important than insisting that much of teaching is a performing art. We must work against entrenched academic attitudes which are as irrational as those which subject matter specialists hold toward courses in education. "Yes," I hear someone say. "Sophists sound the same today as in the past." But what gave the sophists a bad name was the shoddiness of their product, not the effectiveness of their delivery. The

Socratic dialogues owe much to sophism and any teacher could learn from the energetic presence that Socrates must have had. We live amidst rhetoric and rhetoricians developed to a high degree and supported by lavish budgets. The waste of good performances on poor products is a defect of our age. Nevertheless, teachers are in the performing arts and they can compete badly or ably depending on how they choose to develop their skills. Convinced as teachers should be that they are not trying to peddle nostrums and shoddy merchandise, they should press harder to develop skills to win a hearing. Since it is the lives of students that teachers would affect, they should be willing to expend a great deal of energy to perfect their performances.

The teacher without strong convictions about developing the performing aspects of teaching inclines toward presentations which are undramatic, short on gimmickery and devoid of physical presence. Voice, gesture, presence—and occasional words or numbers written on a board—are all that most teachers work with most of the time. If we do not develop the way we use them, do not overcome our inhibitions about performance, do not have the energy to perform, we deprive ourselves of the little we have to gain and hold attention. And if we do not believe, as teachers, that we have the means, in ourselves and through others, of detecting the bogus in our performance, then we should not feel qualified to step before a class.

Some members of this generation are disposed to argue against the presence of the teacher. The modern mood is to get the teacher off a stage he has dominated too long. Part of this mood is a common reaction to hucksterism but part is resentment of the authoritarian pose teachers maintain. The mood is healthy, for it reminds teachers that their performances are but a part of what inclines students to learn. I think performance is insufficiently recognized as the motivating part. If the classroom is going to be used in the standard way—teacher here, students there—then the impact of the performance, immediate stimulation, and continuing motivation are almost everything. Facts can be gathered and reinforced out of books, discussion engaged in after class, further questions explored in the library. It is the energies a teacher arouses by his presence that set learning in motion and keep it going after class. Even if the classroom is to be reorganized with the teacher giving up the principal actor's role and becoming part of the cast, there is no less call upon the teacher's energy. Energy of another kind will be needed to keep the teacher's role in balance and to engage in the student-faculty interactions such teaching necessitates.

In any style of teaching, there are great demands upon the teacher's energy. Mental energy is as important as physical energy. A good teacher, like a good scholar, must have an energetic mind. His mind must not rest easy with answers not yet found or with precision not quite reached. The teacher's mind must reach out to other minds, even to those seemingly most cast in stone, to other places and people, to other experiences. A teacher does not have to be both gymnast and encyclopedist. But unless energy is expended in a wide variety of ways, teaching will remain the kind of okay thing students will sort of put up with.

Fourth, variety is another central attribute of effective teaching. In a teacher, as in a musician, virtuosity might be regarded as the development of one style to ultimate perfection. The breadth we associate with good teaching, however, means the virtuoso teacher must be able to handle other styles as well. A virtuoso teacher would have many ways of teaching and a variety of resources for each. But virtuosity is not a term college teachers readily apply to their profession. It connotes too much temperament, too much display, too much brilliance to describe the routine by which so many college teachers earn their daily bread. In order to win wide recognition as a virtuoso, a teacher would probably have to make dullness part of his repertoire.

The need for variety, however, applies to all teachers. What makes the 50-minute hour seem short is often the ability to break it up into smaller segments. Delivery, mood, format, and subject matter give every teacher sufficient means to achieve a varied performance. On the other hand, it is much too easy to let everything come out in unvaried 50-minute chunks.

Every teacher should have (or pick up) enough performance training to have command of the timing, pace, and dynamics of a verbal performance. It is not enough to know when the class begins and approximately when it ends. Any presentation can be broken up into effective time segments. The lecture-within-a-lecture is probably better than the lecture itself. Stopping short occasionally is better than running over all the time. The ability to sense on the spot a lag in attention and intrude into what had been planned is part of a good sense of timing. A talent for taking advantage of audience interest and going beyond the time planned is another part. It is possible (and should not be disdained) to time a performance, not only to fit it into the class period but to see how many topics can be sketched out, how much time allowed to clarify and to fix concepts, how much time left to provide carryover to the next class meeting. If one is afraid of such mechanical timing, it is as good to listen to one's performance and chart its introduction, rise to climax, and movement toward an end. A good teacher may not have to do this often if his day-by-day teaching stays within a fairly uniform range. In fact, the teacher who possesses a good sense of timing probably has done something like this to develop his timing along the way.

The pace of a teacher's delivery also deserves attention. Large classes are probably less successful than small ones because large size increase the numbers of students for whom the class pace is going to be too fast or too slow. A beginning teacher needs feedback to develop a sense of what a generally acceptable pace would be. Many experienced teachers simply talk too fast or too slow, move the class along too deliberately or too rapidly. The same teacher may need to vary his pace with different classes. The presentation of a course can speed up and slow down within the daily framework as it does over the length of a term. The teacher has command of these factors and should develop his ability to use them to facilitate learning.

Timing and pace are part of the dynamics of a teacher's performance. The voice itself has greater range than most teachers use, even in such simple matters as emphasis. Teachers can be sure that students don't hear everything that is being said. A command of emphasis and a variety of ways of showing emphasis leave less to chance than a delivery having only those inflections the language itself provides. Teachers can and should thunder and whisper if

44

doing so will get a point across. Subtle and broad gestures, physical movement, the willingness to get up from the desk or away from the lectern can also help fix attention, stimulate learning. Performance develops out of practice, not only before students but on audio or video tape, through which one can gain an accurate idea of his practices. Guidance can be also furnished by colleagues—students and faculty—until the teacher reaches the point where he is reasonably adept at sensing the effectiveness of his ordinary classroom delivery.

A variety of moods—even uncommon ones—are useful to the teacher. The prevailing mood of a classroom is probably that of earnest effort. No wonder that humor, irony, and displays of temperament are welcomed by students. The moods of an eccentric genius like George Lyman Kittredge could be terrifying in their impact, but they were unforgettable for the student who felt them. More important, they were not the whole man. The perpetual comic loses his effectiveness as a teacher as does the man or woman who is a chronic scold. The teacher who never lets a mood show may achieve a remarkably consistent image of serious devotion to his subject, but he probably has less impact than he would if his mood were set off by evidences of humanity as well as of scholarship. One of the most important lessons I ever learned from a college teacher (and I have had it reinforced by a number of exceptional teachers) is that an educated person can treat serious things lightly without destroying their worth or indicating that they need to be taken lightly all the time.

A teacher should seek variety in the subjects and arrangements that define his work. The same classes, taught year after year by the same professor, are almost certain to be debilitating to students and teachers alike. Even teaching in the same department is probably not as good for teachers as the universality of the practice might suggest. Teachers need new contexts in the format of classes, the subject matter being taught, and the immediate environment of their teaching. Institutional flexibility should provide varied opportunities to keep a teacher from going stale.

Fifth, though it may seem too small a detail to be included among these general observations, the use of examples and illustrations is too important to be left out. One of my most memorable classroom experiences involved watching a college professor bet his brains against the laws of physics. Standing on one side of a cavernous auditorium, he held to his forehead an iron ball attached by a long cable to the ceiling. He let it go and then stood unmoving as the ball swung across the room and back. It did not, as the laws of motion said it would not, bash his brains out. The students were impressed, relieved, and faintly disappointed.

Such demonstrations are somewhat suspect in the sciences today. Demonstrations get in the way, one physicist told me. Students remember the gimmicks but do not grasp the principles. There is a much older objection, rooted in the attractiveness of the Platonic world, where the sensory is inferior to the abstract, the world of things lower than the world of ideas, mathematics the means by which one rises out of the prison of his senses. These statements are all true, but they are only partial truth as regards transactions between teacher and student. The best witness for the incompleteness of that truth is Socrates himself. It is an important moment when the student realizes that the Socratic dialogues do not talk just about the abstractions—beauty, justice, virtue—but about pipemakers and charioteers, bees and horses, plows and pots, beds and bed-makers. As much as Socrates was concerned with helping the young to perceive truth, he was always drawing upon the particulars of experience and constantly turning to illustration and example.

Much college teaching suffers by being disconnected from doing. Too much is expected of the student whose body and mind are passive. The teacher of physical skills is fortunate in being able to demonstrate by doing, and to ask the student to try to follow his example. A ski instructor, for example, tells his pupils, "It's all in the knees." Then he describes how he wants his students to edge into the hill, putting their knees so, their upper body thus. Then he's off slowly in the traverse leaving the group to transfer what they have seen into physical positions until they can see the terrain with their knees.

At least two general principles can be drawn from that simple illustration. The first is the necessity, and the difficulty, of translating something to be learned into something the learner can do. If we wanted to squeeze all learning into this framework, we would invent "behavioral objectives" and insist that all teaching fit the concept. If we maintain a broader view of teaching, we can take the example of the ski instructor for what it is worth and resist the jargon of conceptualization. Not all learning translates immediately, or ever, into action, just as all learning objectives cannot be described in terms of behavior. The second principle is the indispensability of examples. At some remove from the ski slopes is the language classroom. But hearing a speaker, watching the positioning of the lips, and practicing in the language laboratory all take advantage of examples. Even in studying literature, the need for examples and illustration never diminishes. "See this in the mind's eye," the metaphor asks. Teachers of verbal disciplines may get impatient with examples, as college teachers often disdain illustrations, visual aids, and consider them suitable to lower level classes but not to higher education. Teachers should not reject these techniques. Literature succeeds insofar as it does what Conrad insists is the duty of literature: "to make you hear, to make you feel—it is, before all, to make you *see*. That—and no more, and it is everything."[4] The world needs teachers who can exemplify and illustrate and demonstrate so that the student may understand.

Sixth, however it comes and is maintained, enthusiasm is essential. Students want teachers not only to care about what they are doing but to show that concern. Part of a teacher's enthusiasm is probably grounded in liking people even though this liking may be strongly tempered by a desire to improve them. If all scholars were teachers and all teachers scholars, there would be no argument as to whether we teach subjects or teach students. This is a silly argument but, by its existence, it lays claim to our attention. Students do get in the way of the pursuit of subjects, but one way of catching students is to get excited about one's subject matter. Teachers do teach students, and if working with students is not something a prospective college teacher has enthusiasm for, he should probably

---

[4] Preface to *The Nigger of the Narcissus* (New York: Harper and Brothers, 1951), p. xl.

be counseled into a different occupation. Mrs. Louis Agassiz described her husband in this fashion:

> Teaching was a passion with him, and his power over his pupils might be measured by his own enthusiasm. He was intellectually, as well as socially, a democrat, in the best sense. He delighted to scatter broadcast the highest results of thought and research and to adapt them even to the youngest and most uninformed minds. In his later American travels he would talk of glacial phenomena to the driver of a country stagecoach among the mountains or to some workman, splitting rock at the roadside, with as much earnestness as if he had been discussing problems with a brother geologist; he would take the common fisherman into his scientific confidence, telling him the intimate secrets of fish culture or fish embryology, till the man in his turn grew enthusiastic and began to pour out information from the stores of his own rough and untaught habits of observation. Agassiz's general faith in the susceptibility of the popular intelligence, however untaught, to the highest truths of nature was contagious, and he created or developed that in which he believed.[5]

Liking for people and for scholarly work may not be manifested in overt enthusiasm, particularly by the young teacher. Insecurity may lead to defensive withdrawal or to a teaching posture which keeps such tight control over the course that little room exists for arousing interest. Arrogance, aloofness, and impersonality may be the beginning teacher's responses to not being sure of himself as a teacher. Confidence comes with experience. One of the great benefits of confidence is that it permits the teacher to show genuine enthusiasm for his work.

The boring teacher, the bane of all students, is probably fairly bored himself. A sensitive teacher cannot escape being periodically distressed with the sound of his own voice. An insensitive one never really hears himself just as he does not realize his students have stopped listening. For the sensitive teacher, renewal can come from giving up old concerns and embarking on new ones. Or renewal may require removal from teaching for a time until new experiences and learning arouse a strong urge to let someone else know. For

[5] E. C. Agassiz (Ed.), *Louis Agassiz* (Boston: Houghton, Mifflin and Co., 1885), II, pp. 207–208.

imperceptive teachers, it may be the anger aroused by a low student rating which fires them to show some zeal for their work.

Seventh, in almost all student questionnaires clarity and organization are among the measures of a teacher's performance. I place them in subordinate position here because I think there are other virtues in teaching more important than clarity and the power to organize. "There are some enterprises," Melville wrote, "in which a careful disorderliness is the true method."[6] The material with which a teacher is concerned may have a great deal to do with how well he succeeds in organizing it. Teachers should feel somewhat uneasy if all the things they deal with come out in neat lists, outlines, or classifications. Teachers may take some advantage of the ephemeral, oral form of teaching, of its immediate presentation before students, to leave some things uncounted and unclassified. Students, after all, should be involved in the process of defining, relating, and analyzing their subject to give it order.

Nevertheless, the teacher who merely rambles without some sense of design probably confuses himself as well as his students. Similarly, even well organized teachers fall short if they fail to communicate the value of organizing materials or give students no sense of the larger purpose served by systematizing in an elementary fashion. And the teacher who can only clarify in his own terms rather than in the terms of his students is not likely to inspire them to try to clarify and organize on their own.

Simplification is one of the essential reasons for organizing, one of the best ways of clarifying. An experienced teacher may be distinguished from a beginning teacher by how much he has thrown away. Everything seems important to the person who has just learned it. Teachers of physical skills often seem to have an uncanny ability to spot simple matters of physical movement which affect a tennis stroke or a golf swing. They probably develop this ability through many observations aimed at identifying a few vital particulars. My admiration still remains for a French teacher who had sorted through the complexities of French grammar (and of grammar textbooks) to arrive at a comparatively few things that *must* be

---

[6] *Moby Dick* (New York: Collier Books, 1962), p. 374.

known. He went over these in a class quickly and was free to talk about many matters of greater interest than grammar which sometimes seemed to be leading us away from our tasks. It turned out that they did not, for if we did learn what he said had to be learned, the rest followed. The hard work of sorting out, which the students could not do with an unfamiliar language, had been done by the teacher. He left the student free to concentrate on those matters which provided the essential framework.

While I am discussing the power to clarify and to organize, let me mention the importance I attach to certain traits of mind. The teacher must know a good many things, just as most teachers are helped by wide and varied experience, and some teachers are helped by the quality of their affective response. It is not always scholarly learning which gets a point across and kindles interest in a student. Effective teaching comes out of the scholar's curiosity, curiosity that has been able to operate in the world as well as in the study. Faculty members sometimes worry that students who evaluate professors fail to place enough weight on scholarly competence. The argument that students cannot judge the breadth, depth, or soundness of a teacher's knowledge has some merit. Still, brilliant professors seem to be about as accurately identified by students as they are by faculty. And though students have fewer ways than faculty members have of judging whether a professor's learning is show or substance, they do have some ways. They read books, compare lectures with textbooks and with information gained from other professors; they talk with other students. Students are impressed, and properly so, with teachers who seem to know a lot of things and who don't pretend to know it all. One of the most painful lessons a new teacher learns is not to pretend to know what he does not know. It takes a good deal of teaching experience before a teacher can say, "I don't know," without some sense of falling short. The teacher's prior experience will probably have included some bluffing, some dispensing of misinformation, and a few instances in which students have looked up facts at variance with what the teacher had taken pains to defend.

But knowing in the common sense—grasp of fact, retention of information, power of recall—is not the only mental power a teacher needs. Quick perception, ability to see relationships, curiosity, imagination, and common sense are equally valuable mental traits. The absence of these qualities may justify a student's complaint that a professor's teaching lacks relevance. Wit is not an absolute requirement, but its presence is almost always an asset. Cognitive powers, shading off into affective ones, may usefully bring a larger measure of sympathy, compassion, and understanding into a teacher's work.

Eighth, honesty appears on evaluation questionnaires prepared by students in such inferential ways as "is well prepared," "presents origin of ideas and concepts," "is fair in grading." Such questions do not pry far into the many ways teachers can fall short of scrupulous honesty. Honesty in the teaching profession, like being well prepared, is probably not an absolute requirement. There are times, as for instance when the teacher confronts a failing student, when exact honesty may not seem to be the best course. But even then, a superior teacher carefully weighs the necessity of confronting painful truth for himself and for his students. Teaching is too often less than it should be because of the drift from absolute honesty that academic practice permits. Over the long run, compromises of this kind defeat both the teacher and his students.

Teaching places an extraordinary demand on being believed in. And since it places those who do not know with those who supposedly do know, teaching also affords extraordinary opportunities for deceit. A professor teaching classes while his major interests are somewhere else is, in this moralistic view, dishonest. A scholar writing books he does not quite believe in for purposes he cannot really defend is also dishonest. A faculty member taking money for research work that serves questionable ends is dishonest. A lecturer faking a class off the top of his head is dishonest. The list is easy to add to and hard to keep within reasonable limits. Honesty may be easier for the teacher if one begins to practice self-restraint early in his career. A teacher in some sense always gives some part of himself to help develop the self of another. One needs a developed self to be able to give. Yet the teacher's self can stand in the way of the development of the student. The less concerned we are with self, the less likely we are to be dishonest in furthering our self-interest.

Perhaps honesty is not the precise word I should be using. My intent is to stress the importance of teaching as a moral act. Admitting error, resisting temptation, responding to conscience, having a conscience, being concerned with right and wrong—these practices are essential to the teacher's morality. But concern with right and wrong is not as common as it might seem. A teacher's fidelity to his subject matter may seem to rule out questions of right or wrong. Higher learning tends to make the pursuit of truth the ultimate right to be justified by the truth it will ultimately reveal. Unfortunately, truth does not arrive every day. Provisional truths must guide us in the hourly conduct of our affairs. A sense of right and wrong may have to serve. This does not mean teachers should develop or adopt some narrow moral standard and measure everything they do by that standard. But they should never set considerations of right and wrong aside for long or let their choices be unaffected by such considerations. The university has earned the contempt of some of its students who detect evidence that right and wrong have little to do with many of the university's operations— athletic programs, treatment of women, acceptance of research contracts, granting of degrees—the list is as long as the hair shirt of the man who makes it up. Teachers in the institution cannot escape by attacking the self-righteousness of student moralists or by falling back on the anonymity of their place in the institution. Teachers have made a bargain with both past and future and they must keep faith with parties to the bargain such as Socrates: "For all that I do is go round and persuade young and old among you not to give so much of your attention to your bodies and your money as to the perfection of your souls."[7] Or Thoreau: "I wanted to live deep and suck out all the marrow of life, to cut a broad swath and shave close, to drive life into a corner, and reduce it to its lowest terms, and, if it proved to be mean, why then to get the whole and genuine meanness of it, and publish its meanness to the world; or if it were sublime, to know it by experience, and be able to give a true account of it in my next excursion. For most men, it appears to me, are in a strange uncertainty about it, whether it is of the devil or of God, and have *somewhat hastily* concluded that it is the chief

[7] Plato, *Apology*, 29E.

52

end of man here to 'glorify God and enjoy him forever.' "[8] Students, too, who have yet to fashion the expressions by which other men may live, are parties to this bargain.

Finally, a wise teacher develops his sense of proportion. He knows more, has more to balance, and balances more skillfully. He also does some things very well: writing, acting, designing structures, digging in the earth, or an active, doing kind of teaching which gets students to start doing things themselves. Teaching of this kind goes beyond subject matter as thinking goes beyond subject matter and beyond action.

Teaching moves toward openness, toward willingness to enter into a mutual experience of learning shared by students and faculty alike. Teaching is simple to do and to keep on doing in a mediocre fashion. But superior teaching makes the same kinds of demands as does any craft or art.

Consider the many ways any lesson may be learned, the myriad purposes to which learning may be put, the complex personalities of individual teachers and learners, the tangle of relationships learning involves. Is it any wonder that learning does not always go well? Is that any reason for not working to make it go better?

[8] *Walden* (Cambridge, Mass.: The Riverside Press, 1957), pp. 62–63.

CHAPTER 4

Evaluating
Teaching

O f the three objectives of the project, evaluation of teaching clearly aroused the greatest interest. Attention has come as much from administrators as from faculty and has been shared by the public involved with higher education. Our booklet, *The Recognition and Evaluation of Teaching,* aroused a strong and continuing response. It has been distributed to faculty members, administrators, and students in almost all colleges and universities in this country and to a scattering abroad.

Why the interest in evaluation of teaching? The foremost reason is the need to give teaching visibility. A reward system which attaches prestige to research for which there is a highly visible and quantifiable measure—publication—leaves faculty members uneasy about fair rewards for teaching. Although faculty members are also uneasy about having evaluators visit their classrooms or letting students make ratings of professors public, most professors are caught between the desire to have their teaching count in the reward system and reluctance to undergo systematic evaluation. Administrators are less hesitant about adopting evaluation systems than are faculty members. Chairmen and deans are already charged with responsibility for seeing that teaching is done well. For their own self-protection, as well as for the good of the institution, they need measures of faculty performance that are fair and reasonably precise. Although some administrators seize upon evaluation as the key to teaching excellence while others back away from the systematization that goes with many evaluation procedures, most administrators support attempts to set criteria forth clearly and to have judgments of performance which will be respected by the faculty.

The current interest in evaluation is linked with accountability, a word that does a disservice by implying that education has not been accountable in the past, and which may be used to justify reduced support of education generally. Nevertheless, the concept springs from a widespread public mood. Both private and public institutions must accept the fact that members of the public are showing interest in what they get for the money they spend. Students have steadily become more aggressive in making similar demands upon institutions. The adoption of student rating systems has been a response to pressures from students and from the public at large.

But judging faculty performance and responding to demands for accountability are only some of the functions evaluation of teaching performs. Development of effective teachers can also be aided by evaluation, and faculty members uneasy about the judgmental aspects of evaluation will often accept its developmental uses. Obviously the ability to evaluate teaching depends on ability to identify important characteristics of teaching performance and supporting activities. Extensive research into various aspects of the use of student responses to judge teaching performance has contributed greatly to understanding of the teaching/learning process. Unless it is altogether true that teachers are born and not made, knowledge we gain about teaching effectiveness can be used in the development of better teachers.

The project's work underscores the lack of faculty development efforts throughout higher education. Under most tenure systems, faculty members undergo a probationary period before being granted tenure. Yet little is done during that probationary period to systematically develop the untenured professor's ability as a teacher. The young professor does not receive much help in developing teaching skill in the graduate school nor is he likely to receive such help later in his career. Evaluation does not necessarily lead to its being used in developing effective teachers, but without some confidence in our ability to identify the elements of good teaching, institutions have one more reason for neglecting this concern.

There are both opportunities and threats implicit in the current emphasis upon evaluation of teaching. Most of my visits to campuses were related to student evaluation. On every visit I found both strong support and strong opposition among the faculty. Soon after the project began, I received through the Washington office of the AAUP, cosponsor of the project, the following letter. I reprint it in its entirety both for its substance and for its tone of expression:

> I am deeply disturbed by the current project of the AAUP, described in the latest issue of *Academe,* February, 1970, concerning improvement of college teaching. No one, of course, is against good teaching. It is a condition so greatly to be desired that any reasonable suggestions for accomplishing it must be given serious attention. Unfortunately, up to now there have been no reasonable suggestions, as far as I am aware, and certainly the two things which the AAUP seems to be suggesting will not bear even cursory examination.
>
> These two things, unless I misread the admittedly rather vague discussion—a vagueness, by the way, all too characteristic of most discussions of educational methods—are the institution of some kind of teacher training for graduate students working for the Ph.D. in course who may in the future go into teaching, and [a] student evaluation form which will be used in consideration of promotion and tenure.
>
> In regard to the first of these, the modern Ph.D. is one of the most rigorous and demanding intellectual exercises to which the human mind is subjected. Its satisfactory completion requires not only a mind of considerably better than average powers of concentration, discrimination, analysis, and synthesis, but a large amount of time devoted to intense mental effort and the accumulation of an immense store of facts and theories requiring long study and memorization. The candidate, particularly if he is to

enter the university world, must be singlemindedly devoted to his subject and willing to give a good part of his life to its service. In order to keep abreast of it and in order that it may remain alive for him, he must continue to study it, and in most cases to engage in at least a measure of scholarly research, though the need for intense and continuous research may perhaps be over-emphasized.

One who is already expending this amount of time and effort in a field which is necessarily the center of his interest cannot reasonably be required to achieve some level of skilled performance in a second field, *entirely unrelated* to his interest, before he is allowed to practice in his chosen area. This is a requirement imposed on no other profession, and which no other profession would tolerate; and no matter how great the benefits might be, the profession of scholarship—already badly underrewarded in comparison with such fields as medicine and law—should not tolerate it either. In point of fact, experience with public school teacher training, which includes such emphasis on methods, indicates that far from being great, the benefits are likely to be undiscernible.

The second suggestion, to employ student evaluations as methods of deciding on promotion and tenure, is in effect a way of compelling the scholar to become an expert in an unrelated field, just as the first is; and like the first, it imposes an unreasonable requirement.

What is really meant by good teaching is the achievement of a technique for putting expert knowledge in an entertaining and amusing way so that the student will be attracted to it and hence learn it more easily. This is surely desirable, but it should be remembered that the student does not normally come to college in order to be entertained and amused by skilled public speakers, but in order to have access to the knowledge of experts in various fields. Taking advantage of this access may require some effort on his part beyond being present on the physical premises —even some effort to understand what he is hearing and participating in through the exercise of his own powers of comprehension, unaided by easy learning techniques. I am not unsympathetic with the student; I have encountered enough examples of inarticulate scholars to know what they are suffering. But neither of your suggested solutions can be considered reasonable as requirements to be imposed on the profession of scholarship, on which, in both sciences and humanities, the development and indeed the life of society now depends.

I have a long-standing admiration for and loyalty to the AAUP, but if these are indeed your present lines of activity, I do not feel that I can in conscience contribute to carrying them out.

There was a nice symmetry in the fact that a year later, as I was moving toward completion of my work, I received a similar letter. This time it was accompanied by a copy of a letter sent to the heads of the sponsoring organizations requesting that my services be terminated. The issue was, once again, evaluation.

These are not representative responses. In fact, they were the only negative responses from among hundreds received. They were useful reminders that evaluating teaching raises a good many instinctive reactions from those who feel that the classroom should be free from outside scrutiny as well as from those who worry about the ways evaluation can disturb the sensitive relationships between student and teacher upon which effective teaching may depend. There are also many legitimate questions about the particulars of evaluating teaching, and there is a very large unanswered question about whether evaluating teaching on a given campus actually leads to improved instruction. It is my firm conclusion that the need for improved undergraduate teaching necessitates improved systems of evaluating teaching including student evaluation and visitation of classes. I further believe that the means for reasonable and effective evaluation of teaching are available to any college or university and that they should be used in decisions about advancement as well as for development of skill in teaching.

John W. Gustad's[1] studies of 1961 and Alexander W. Astin and Calvin B. T. Lee's[2] updating in 1966 provide a wealth of data on how teaching performance is evaluated in various kinds of colleges and universities. In both surveys, chairmen and deans were identified as the major sources of information at all colleges and

[1] *Policies and Practices in Faculty Evaluation* (Washington, D.C.: American Council on Education, 1961).

[2] "Current Practices in the Evaluation and Training of College Teachers," in C. B. T. Lee (Ed.), *Improving College Teaching* (Washington, D.C.: American Council on Education, 1967), pp. 296–311.

universities. Colleagues' opinions, informal student opinions, and committee evaluations were other sources of information used in varying degrees at various institutions. Measures based on student performance—grade distributions, student examination performance, enrollment in elective courses, course syllabi, and examinations—were less frequently used. Self-evaluation was well down the list in both surveys as was alumni opinion. Systematic student ratings and classroom visits were mentioned frequently in 1961, less frequently in 1966. My recent inquiries suggest that the use of systematic student ratings has greatly increased since 1966.

In practice, within individual departments, any combination of these means—in some instance all of them—are employed in judging teaching. Where departments are strong (and that means in all but the smallest four-year colleges and many junior colleges) the chairman has a decisive role through the information he can provide the rest of the departmental faculty and through his own judgment of a teacher's performance. The department level is usually the only level at which firsthand information is available. The chairman may visit classes or colleagues may become acquainted with each other's teaching through visiting, team teaching, or guest lecturing. The achievements of students are also known within the department as are course materials, enrollment data, and the like. In smaller colleges, the dean may exercise some of the functions of the chairman. Everywhere else the dean's function, though important, is to review rather than to make firsthand judgments. But even within the department, much of the basis for judging teaching performance is largely inferential. Judgments are based on appraisals of a colleague's qualities of mind, manner of address, casual conversations with students and other colleagues, research and publications. Some of these may have a bearing upon teaching performance; some may not.

Obviously, the means of judging teaching are not very precise though they may be fairly diverse and they may be applied within a carefully defined framework. To some degree, department chairmen consult with other members of a department on matters which affect individual faculty members' advancement. Commonly, the department is involved in one manner or another in discussions which lead to a formal recommendation. Where consultation procedures are carefully spelled out, adequate provisions are made for review by people or committees outside the department, and proper grievance procedures are established, the evaluation system may work reasonably well despite reliance on informal practices and imprecise measures. To a marked degree, members of the academic community seem to prefer personal, informal, admittedly subjective, and supposedly humane ways of looking at advancement. Just as faculty members may lose favor by scrambling after promotion, so the advancement process may lose favor if it moves toward precise, systematized, and impersonal means of passing on a colleague's qualifications. My work makes me think that faculty members may be moving toward more firmly defined practices and policies. The current, strong interest in evaluation of teaching is an indication of such a movement.

General procedures aside, what possibilities for adding sources of information about the effectiveness of teaching and increasing the reliability of such sources are there? Classroom visitation, self-appraisal, review of course materials and data, student opinion, and measures of student achievements are all used as sources of data in addition to that commonly furnished by department chairmen and colleagues. The use of sophisticated observation techniques by trained evaluators and analysis of teachers' effectiveness in relation to students' learning should also be mentioned. Student opinion, reliably gathered and wisely used, probably has the best chance of providing useful data and of being incorporated into institutional practices.

Let us look briefly at each of these possibilities. There is no substitute for actual observation of a teacher in a classroom for judging how well he does this aspect of his job. That does not mean, however, that visiting will provide a reliable measure. A visitor can ascertain elementary but important things with reasonable objectivity such as whether the teacher can be heard, whether his material is organized, whether he speaks too rapidly or too slowly, and whether he entertains and answers questions. The visitor can also observe students in the class and infer some things about how the teacher is coming across. In a single visit, he cannot precisely tell whether one performance is typical of all, whether a visitor's presence adversely or favorably affects the teacher's performance, or whether the students' response that day accords with their overall performance. Nor can the visitor tell how classroom performance relates to the work of teaching and learning which goes on outside. But the things which cannot be known or can be known only imperfectly should not prevent us from acknowledging the usefulness of classroom visitation.

As yet faculty members are not very receptive to visits. A chairman may look in upon graduate assistants but it is much less common for him to visit senior colleagues. The reasons for resistance are many. Suspicions toward the visitor's intentions, uneasiness caused by the presence of a stranger in the classroom, violation of dignity or professional standing, and doubts about the outcome of the observation are some of the reasons commonly cited. Even if one sets these objections aside, extensive visiting requires a good deal of time. There are substantial enough reasons on both sides to raise doubts that visiting classes will be widely adopted as an evaluation procedure. That does not mean visiting is not a good idea or that opening up the classroom is not a good way to begin to improve teaching.

The availability of recording devices seems to improve the possibilities for unobtrusive observation. Any suggestion that these devices be used, however, may easily arouse the suspicions of the faculty. How does such evaluation stop short of policing the thought content of a course? There is a legitimate fear of technology's penchant for violating privacy. Whether these fears are justified or not, an examination of the use made of such devices does not indicate they will be readily adopted. Tape recorders have been easily available for fifteen years, yet one hears very rarely of their being used systematically by faculty or administrators to record instruction. Video tape adds another dimension and is sometimes used in training public school teachers, but video tape is still a long way from being incorporated into evaluation of college teaching. The conclusion I am forced to draw is that as useful as personally visiting or recording performances by audio or video tape appears to be, faculty resistance to use of these techniques in evaluative ways works against their being widely adopted.

Self-appraisal, like visiting, has its uses. This time, suspicions about it come from the administrative side, rather than from the faculty. Administrators are hesitant, justifiably I think, to place too much reliance on self-observations. Their hesitation is supported, within the context of the reward system, because research to some degree receives objective assessment from outside scholars. Within the faculty, self-appraisal of teaching is often held in low esteem; it is widely held that such measures should not be necessary for trained professionals. I do not share this disdain. A searching self-evaluation can be a source of information and of a resolve to improve one's skill. But I do not think such subjective data will be regarded as a substantial addition to evaluation processes which seem most in need of objective data.

Course materials and data are widely used as a second order of materials for judging teaching performance. Assessments come almost always through a department chairman or dean and depend heavily on that individual's interpretation of the data. The chances for imprecise use of such materials are great but they provide information which can be compared within a department and which has some degree of comparability outside. Such materials can usefully be divided into those which say something about the teacher's competence—results of examinations, kinds of courses taught, enrollments in elective classes, course syllabi and other materials—and those which affect the teacher's competence—number of students, size of classes, and level of classes. Careful use of this information affords a chairman a measure of how difficult a task the individual has been assigned and how well or with how little complaint he has done it. Certainly, fairness and precision should be sought in using such measures, but they are probably chiefly important as supplementary data.

Measures of student achievement remain the philosopher's stone in evaluating teaching. If it were possible to put students into the before and after poses that sell hair pieces and reducing aids, evaluation would be an easy thing. But teaching and learning are very difficult to isolate. Studies that have attempted to do so cast some doubt on the weight to be given to classroom teaching in accounting for learning. Within the institutional context, the forces that bear upon a student's learning in any class are probably as wide as his range of activities and thoughts during the quarter. If we give due importance to what the student brings with him before he begins a class, the calculations become even more difficult. Though it might be possible to isolate relevant learning factors under carefully controlled conditions, it seems unlikely that these conditions could be achieved with respect to large numbers of classes, teachers, and students.

The popularity of behavioral objectives has given some support to attempts to measure a teacher's effectiveness by how well his students achieve defined objectives. But behavioral objectives apply, in a strict sense, only to portions of teaching. Where they do apply, the before and after of objective testing already affords considerable data. Even in courses in which student achievements are objectively measured, factors other than course materials and the teacher's activities have a bearing upon the students' achievements. In such courses, the teacher may become relatively less important as a performer and more important as a designer of learning devices. There is no reason teachers should not function in this way and be judged accordingly. It would still be necessary to evaluate teaching in which the teacher's presence in the classroom—his performance—is assumed to further learning.

Trying to identify the precise effectiveness of a teacher by measuring the students' learning may cast doubt on the premises from which most college instruction proceeds: that teachers in classrooms are a means of learning. Classroom teaching must be viewed skeptically but I have found no evidence that all aspects of the most common arrangements for teaching and learning are wrong. There is still some point in trying to evaluate teaching by carefully examining the particulars of the teacher's classroom performance.

Other possibilities for evaluation depend largely on trained observers working closely with students and teachers. The trained observer in a classroom is probably more capable of identifying factors critical to learning than is the casual visitor. Given the opportunity that repeated observations and correlations with student responses and achievements provide, much can be learned. It is even possible that knowledge gained under laboratory conditions can be applied to nonlaboratory classes. However, that step is not easy to make, and experiments of this kind have had most practical use in applications to student response techniques. Video tape adds to the sophistication with which teaching behavior can be observed, and the presence of data-processing equipment theoretically makes possible the analysis of masses of data on such behavior and correlation with data on learning behaviors of students. Meanwhile, however, the profession has the need to use means of evaluation nearer at hand.

In comparison with other possibilities, carefully gathered student opinion ranks high as a source of data. The reasons are practical as well as theoretical. We need input that can be fairly easily gathered and that can be accepted and even respected by faculty members. It is also useful to have data which have some degree of cross-comparability and which can be made visible to the university community. Theoretical considerations suggest the need for firsthand input rather than inferential information and input from sources close to, if not right at, the point of learning. Student evaluation meets all these specifications and in addition rests on a substantial basis of careful investigation and refinement of instruments and techniques.

My conclusions are as follows:

First, considering the variety of teachers and students and their diversity of talents, training, and inclinations, the profession should be receptive to all those means by which a teacher might gain insight into his courses and manner of teaching.

Second, the present system of evaluating faculty performance stresses judgment more than development, secrecy rather than openness, and the informal, inferential, and subjective judgment of teaching rather than the systematic, firsthand, and objective.

Third, since departments and department chairmen are so important in the practices of evaluating faculty, the department chairman should involve all members of the department in frequent review and written formulation of the criteria and procedures for promotion and tenure.

Fourth, systematic student evaluation is the most practical and substantial addition to the means now being used to evaluate faculty performance as teachers. Wisely formulated, wisely administered, and wisely used, student evaluation can be useful to improving teaching in a number of ways.

Fifth, student input should constitute a substantial part of the data on which decisions of a faculty member's competence as a teacher are based. This does not set aside the importance of input from other sources in judging teaching competence, nor does it imply that effective teaching is the sole measure of a faculty member's competence. Student evaluation of teaching should play an important part in decisions on retention, tenure, and promotion.

Sixth, cooperation among students, faculty and administrators is vital to the success of student evaluation, and continuing support is necessary for continuing success.

Seventh, student evaluation should be part of broader attempts to enhance teaching in forms that attempt to reach all teachers and all students, that are continuing rather than sporadic, that focus upon the interaction between teacher and student, and which give the student responsibility for and active participation in his own education.

Many questions have been raised about the reliability and results of student evaluation. The most persistent questions are whether characteristics of good teaching can be identified, whether student ratings reveal anything other than a teacher's popularity, whether teachers change as a result of ratings, and whether the use of student ratings improves teaching.

All these questions can fairly be answered yes.

There seems to me to be no question that characteristics of effective teaching can be identified. This accords with the results of hundreds of studies and the practical sense of generations of teachers. Whether a group of faculty and students sit around a table and decide what are the most important characteristics of effective classroom performance or a careful study uses factor analysis to arrive at most significant characteristics, the results do not vary greatly. As one reads the literature which describes such studies or examines hundreds of student questionnaires, he is struck by the recurrence of common questions. Aside from the wisdom of students and faculty sitting down together to think about the important characteristics of teaching, a standardized form could be used by colleges and universities wishing to undertake responsible student evaluations. The items which frequently appear on carefully composed questionnaires are important in themselves and they are questions to which students are able to give a response. No good questionnaire can omit specific items about (1) the teacher's command of the subject, (2) the teacher's ability to organize, explain, and clarify, (3) the teacher's ability to arouse and sustain interest, (4) the teacher's willingness to entertain ideas other than his own, and (5) the teacher's ability to establish rapport with a class and with individual students. Specific questions should deal with activities indicative of the more general characteristic. For example, presenting facts and concepts from related fields and citing sources of current information indicate a teacher's command of his subject. A distinctive style of presentation, ability to dramatize portions of a lecture, and displays of enthusiasm and energy offer evidence of ability to arouse interest. There are mysteries in teaching but they have to do with the personal characteristics of student and teacher more than with the basic means by which a teacher goes about his task. Students are singularly important observers because they are the ones upon whom teaching is to have an effect. Their responses to the questions which can be asked about a teacher's performance provide valuable and reliable data.

Why is there so much hesitation about using this kind of feedback? One important but often unacknowledged reason is that many teachers think of teaching as a personal, often idiosyncratic, art which should not be made to suffer simplistic examination. As a humanist, I sympathize with my colleagues who, as a group, are much more hostile to systematic attempts to evaluate teaching than are engineers or professors in colleges of business. Unlike my most resistant colleagues, however, I think teaching is neither such a fragile art that it can be harmed by inquiry nor so complex a craft, as I have seen it practiced, that most teachers' performances could not be improved through attention to fundamentals.

Another common argument against evaluation begins by citing some aimless, arrogant, dull, or quirky teacher who turned out to be the one best teacher some person ever had. We should be suspicious of "turned out to be" arguments but the possibility might be acknowledged. That does not necessarily mean, however, that the basic characteristics of teaching are flouted by these successful teachers. The monumentally dull professor may arouse and sustain interest in the same way that any morbidly exaggerated human characteristic holds our attention. The arrogant professor may have had such command of the subject or possessed such energy and zeal that he forced learning as one of the prices of resisting him. Teaching does not succeed by just one trait even though marked development of some one technique may make it seem so.

Further, the characteristics discussed here are performance characteristics, limited to what goes on in class. The importance of these characteristics is based on the assumption that the classroom interchange between teacher and student fosters learning. As long as professors meet with students two, three, or four times a week over a quarter or a semester supposedly to facilitate learning, it is fair and reasonable to examine the particulars of that performance. I do not mean to slight other aspects vital to classroom performance, such as the preparation of material, skillful testing, assistance outside of class, and the nature of assignments and exercises. Any thorough evaluation would find ways of assessing these, too. Student input can be useful and accurate in measuring many facets of teaching. One thing the effective teacher steadily does, either by informal or formal questioning, is to inquire about how various aspects of the course are working. There is a strong likelihood that teachers who pay attention to the details of effective classroom performance also pay attention to the equally important aspects of teaching which go on outside class.

Student ratings will never completely overcome the charge that they are only popularity contests. There is probably an ingrained resistance to formal teaching as strong at times as the inclination to learn. The American school structure has certainly conditioned students to resist learning by taking children away from the joyful learning of play and putting them under the constraints of classes, teachers, and subjects. College professors should have shaken off the effects of that experience or, in the process of becoming teachers, they should have been exposed to enough ancient or current learning theory to opt for pleasure and reward as better incentives to learning than punishment and fear. Perhaps the defective graduate education they go through conditions them to suspect even their own teaching methods when they threaten to arouse popular enthusiasm.

Defensible student evaluation instruments do not really single out popularity in its meretricious sense nor are students likely to answer a set of specific questions only in terms of the professor's popular appeal. The aim of specific, multiple questions is to get information about different aspects of a teacher's performance. Scrutiny of thousands of questionnaires at perhaps the easiest point for testing the popularity hypothesis—the correlation between favorable grades and favorable responses—repeatedly shows no correlation. The reason for this lack of correlation probably lies in the nature of the questionnaires and the students who answer them. If one wished to register only a general liking for a popular professor, he would have to shift every question from the specific point queried to the general question "do I like the teacher?" The evidence does not support the popular belief that students' ratings of professors are distorted by the meretricious effects of popularity.

The distrust of professors' popular appeal is based on the assumption that popularity is bad. Perhaps professors as a group dissociate themselves from popularity. This is a matter of some importance if we are to take seriously the question of whether popularity in teaching has good or bad effects. The usual argument is that the popular professor's success is in some degree dependent upon his espousing false doctrines. Granting this possibility, I can find no convincing evidence that the unpopular professor is a sure purveyor of truth. We are not dealing with clear-cut distinctions supported by general evidence or by the weight of actual examples. Meanwhile, a good deal of harm is done when a suspicion toward popularity condones teaching that has no impact at all or when some teachers turn away from the legitimate task of gaining the passionate attention of large numbers of students. If we would separate the professor of false doctrines from the ones who strenuously try to remain conversant with truth, we and they must be willing to have their teaching examined.

The last two questions are more difficult. The weight of evidence, most of it subjective, supports a belief that teachers are changed for the better by student ratings and that teaching, in that respect, probably improves. It is difficult to make an exact accounting in these matters. We can try, as a number of institutions have done, to ask the teachers themselves whether, and in what ways, they think student ratings have changed them. The results seem to favor the view that ratings have positive effects on most. We can infer that if a majority of individual faculty members think they have improved as teachers, a general improvement must have taken place. Unfortunately, there are few places where ratings have remained constant over a number of years and where careful attempts have been made to measure the effects.

Perhaps there will never be hard evidence to prove that student evaluations improve teaching. At the very least, student ratings call attention to teaching and exert pressure upon faculty members to perform at a minimum level. The ratings themselves may be less important than the discussions they provoke, the power they have to make teaching a live issue on campus, and the favorable effects they may have on the general climate for learning. Ratings may also lead to other activities in support of teaching. Acceptance of a rating system as part of advancement procedures may lead faculty members to press for specific administrative support of the development of teaching skills. And where student ratings are an innovation on campus, they may open the door for other innovations in teaching procedures, class structures, and the like.

If student ratings are forced upon the faculty or exist outside the university structure as in the past at Berkeley and Harvard, the faculty may adopt a stance that somewhat reverses ordinary values—the lower the faculty member's rating by the students, the higher his standing with the faculty. Where ratings intensify divisions between faculty and students, or seem to be used by an administration against the faculty, no very good outcomes can be foreseen. Student ratings are no panacea for improving teaching. Effects vary from campus to campus, as they vary from individual to individual. At one time, usually at inception, they may be very effective. At other times, often after they have been in use for a number of years, their effects may diminish. But this can be said of any continuing practice, including teaching. On balance, student evaluation of teaching seems to contribute important data to the reward system that is not easily available from other sources and it calls attention to faculty performance in a way that is likely to produce favorable results.

Many questions continue to arise about student evaluation. What are the best forms? Is a campuswide instrument best or should various instruments be devised to fit departments? Should results be published? Should participation in student ratings be mandatory for the faculty? Should student ratings be used in decisions on promotion and tenure? If so, how much weight should they be given and in what way should the data be incorporated into the decision making process? How often should classes be evaluated? Who should be responsible for establishing and maintaining a rating system?

There are general answers to many of these questions,[3] but individual colleges must still seek answers most satisfactory to them. Students ratings are not a simple matter to be dismissed as a student fad or accepted in an unmindful way. It is to the students' credit that the rating systems in effect in a majority of colleges and universities show such a high degree of care in the construction of questionnaires and the gathering of data. Many show sophistication and literary skill in describing what goes on in college classrooms. For the most part, this has been accomplished without faculty tutoring or administrative support and with considerable tact, grace, wit, and, when necessary, assertion of students' rights to register opinions on such an important activity as teaching.

The chief difficulty students face in trying to carry out a respectable course of faculty evaluation is that of maintaining the

[3] Eble, pp. 21–33.

70

interest of the student body and commanding the necessary time and energy from the small group of students who do the major work connected with evaluation. It is necessary, if a student evaluation is to get convincing data, to maintain a high level of response from the students. Experience seems to show that participation is high when an evaluation process first begins and drops away as the system continues. Experience also shows that a certain group of students may maintain a superior system for a number of years only to have it deteriorate under the direction of another group of students. Both conditions underline the need for faculty and administration to lend a hand and contribute what the continuity of the faculty and the financial and directive support of the administration can provide. If we consider student ratings a valuable contribution to the maintenance of effective teaching, the faculty and administration can afford to invest support for the enterprise. This can probably not, and should not, be accomplished by taking evaluation away from the students or by co-opting them into doing the faculty's or administration's work. But examples are plentiful—Princeton, the University of Washington, the University of Massachusetts, Bowling Green, the University of Utah—in which cooperative programs supported by students, faculty, and administration are sustaining the positive effects of a student rating system.

Perhaps the most encompassing, carefully developed system using student ratings is the one established at Princeton and described at some length in the Evaluation booklet.[4] After three years of campuswide use, the Committee on the Course of Study recommended that the program be continued for another three years. The changes the Committee suggested add to what the academic community is beginning to know about the operation of a system over a longer period of time. The Committee recommended that the course evaluation questionnaires be shortened and that individual student's comments on courses be solicited independently of the tabulated responses (primarily for the benefit of the instructor). Shortening of the basic form may make it possible to maintain participation near the 75 per cent level. It was also noted that students

[4] *Ibid.,* pp. 50–61.

and faculty might be suffering from "evaluation fatigue." This phenomenon is observable elsewhere. At the University of Utah, where a campuswide published evaluation was set up in 1968 and achieved excellent results, other evaluations began springing up. By 1970, there was clearly too much evaluation going on. The Princeton report recommended cutting back in order to make the process more important to all concerned. Campuswide surveys need not be annual if a careful survey is conducted to cover all colleges and departments over a period of two or three or four years. A general survey can wisely exclude very small classes or classes taught in ways unsuited to the survey techniques. Overlapping evaluations can be eliminated. What is necessary is careful, campuswide, cooperative management of evaluations in the best interests of both student and faculty.

It would be a real loss if the interest in student evaluation declined and the expertise that has been gained in developing instruments and procedures and the knowledge about teaching that came out of this activity were no longer put to use. That decline would likely result from the failure of students, faculty, or administration to exercise continuing responsibility, or from shortcomings that can be recognized and remedied. Evaluating teaching, including the use of student ratings, is not a system or process that can be put into effect and thereafter run effortlessly and efficiently. If it is to retain the humane characteristics faculties rightly prize, evaluation must be constantly examined, refined, and modified to fit contexts which are always changing. The end—excellent teaching— may remain constant, but the means for achieving it require the resourcefulness of the entire campus community to develop techniques which work best at any given time.

CHAPTER 5

What Students Want

The emphasis upon student evaluation of faculty doubtless rises out of student unrest of the past decade. Evaluation is one of the few formal ways students have of indicating to the faculty what they want. Although good student evaluation forms are specific about teaching performance, they cover a limited range of what students expect from the college experience. Students deliberately hide as well as reveal their mysteries; they change their minds; they put faculty members on. The term *college students* applies to such numbers and varieties that it is no longer possible to make easy generalizations about college age youth. Nevertheless, we can conjecture about what, in a larger sense, the students want. Generalizations will abound in this chapter but they will be made with reservations and with some specific warnings about the distortions these generalizations may involve.

Helpful to this inquiry is a large and highly respectable body of scholarly work. The studies of most direct interest are those which examine the values students hold and the ways colleges may have affected such values. These studies, beginning with Philip

Jacob's[1] *Changing Values in College: An Exploratory Study of the Impact of College Teaching,* constitute a large body of literature. They look at the question posed in this chapter from the perspective of how students are affected by the college experience. In examining these effects, most of these studies touch upon student desires and aspirations.

Kenneth A. Feldman and Theodore M. Newcomb in *The Impact of College on Students* conclude that the college experience results in few changes in the personal characteristics of students and that the changes which do take place are widespread among students on many different campuses but neither universal nor radical.[2] Among the changes careful studies seem to detect are a decrease in conservatism and dogmatism, increased interest in intellectual pursuits and capacities for independence, dominance, and self-confidence, and a greater readiness to express rather than to inhibit impulses. Unfortunately, few studies make any attempt to match observations of college youth with observations of noncollege youth of the same age. Nor do the mass studies sufficiently reflect significant variations among students. Well-focused studies seem to indicate that the college experience tends to strengthen values students have when they enter college. The college influences which are particularly potent are those which match the readiness of the students to be influenced in particular ways.

I cite Newcomb's cautious conclusions because they are based on a large body of previous research and because they contrast sharply with what other writers proclaim as the values of youth. Charles Reich's *The Greening of America* and Theodore Roszak's *The Counter-Culture* are probably the best known among current books. Every academic year there is a new set of articles and books analyzing current campus crises or generalizing on what the youth movement portends for the future. Such materials are not to be dismissed out of hand though it is fair to say they offer more provocation than proof.

Other sources of data are opinion polls which sample what students are thinking. Polls cover various segments of the student

[1] New York: Harper and Brothers, 1957.
[2] San Francisco: Jossey-Bass, 1969.

74

population along with large overall samplings. These surveys are never complete enough or precise enough to be convincing but they are sources of interesting information. In general, pollsters find that the majority of students are satisfied with their college experience. A winter 1968–1969 poll, for example, revealed that only 4 per cent of seniors and 2 per cent of freshmen found higher education "basically unsound—needs much overhauling," while 19 per cent of seniors and 32 per cent of freshmen found it "basically sound— essentially good."[3] "Polls of student opinion," the Scranton report concluded, "do not, in fact, indicate widespread discontent with higher education."[4] The *Fortune* survey "What They Believe" identified 20 per cent of the students as "forerunners," interested in exploring the world, critical, identity-seeking, concerned with life style, and, by implication, dissatisfied with higher education as it is.[5]

What these student opinions seem to indicate is somewhat contradictory. On the one hand, loud voices and determined actions are telling us that college and university education, in one respect and another, must change; on the other, a silent-until-polled majority is saying that things are generally better than all right. The contradiction is not only a matter of prevailing versus minority opinion. As the Scranton report makes clear, campus protests have been concerned with the "great primary issues" of racism, the war in Vietnam, and denial of personal freedom. In looking at dissatisfaction with the university itself, the report concludes: "Though at times this issue has been expressed in protests over curriculum and the nonretention of popular teachers, the overwhelming majority of university-related protests have dealt with school regulations affecting students, with the role of students in making these regulations, and more generally with the quality of student life, living facilities, and food service."[6]

It should not be surprising that most students generally ap-

[3] Reported in "The Scranton Report, Text of the Findings of the President's Commission on Campus Unrest," *The Chronicle of Higher Education,* Oct. 5, 1970, p. 8.

[4] *Ibid.,* p. 9.

[5] January 1969, *79*(1), 70–71, 179–181.

[6] Scranton Report, p. 8.

prove of an academic experience which requires limited personal involvement and which follows a regular, patterned, and ultimately certified process toward almost certain economic and cultural benefits. Only large dislocations in society are likely to initiate an era when, according to Kenneth Keniston, "upward mobility, career success, prestige, money, family-togetherness, no longer serve to animate a growing minority of students."[7]

The demands of these students are often vague when they deal with academic concerns. Often these demands are associated with general political activism, such as the right to representation on faculty committees, and they are usually negative, such as general criticisms of grades and bad teachers. Faculty members can, therefore, fairly easily ignore student criticism. Or faculties can make the easy concession of giving the students a voice and then being dismayed either at the lack of alternatives students propose or at the fitful interest students maintain. Providing alternatives and maintaining interest are a teacher's business just as helping students to realize vaguely felt desires should be among a teacher's foremost aims. There is no one set of things all students want. Even general human wants—love, respect, security, freedom—have different degrees of value for different students. In a general way, some students, loud enough to be heard and colorful enough to engage the media, want to do their own thing, to blow their minds, to stamp out war, disease and poverty, to shock their elders, to pull down institutions, and to be able to buy pot legally. It is probably just as valid to say that a large number of students want to get passing grades, not work too hard, get some fun out of life, honor their fathers and mothers, support their local institutions, and be able to buy panty hose, Certs, and Wayne Newton records at the supermarket.

The professor as teacher cannot avoid facing general manifestations of student desires. But our discussion from this point on will deal only with some student desires which have a close relationship to learning and teaching and which should affect teaching

[7] "What's Bugging the Students," in David C. Nichols (Ed.), *Perspectives on Campus Tensions* (Washington, D.C.: American Council on Education, 1970), p. 63.

practices. These desires are: relevance, participation in important decisions affecting educational policies and practices, acknowledgment of natural youthful inclinations, and respect for various values embodied in the youth culture.

No word has been more abused in student-faculty discussions of teaching than *relevance*. The word has become a mere signal. As such, the term is not to be trusted whether used by students or faculty. But it is always a loss when a good word falls into disrepute, when the word's reputation has to be acknowledged before one feels free to use it. *Relevance* is too good a word to abandon, and the present state of its usage is germane, that is, relevant, to this discussion.

Students are right when they ask for relevance in teaching because relevance is a fundamental necessity of learning wherever and whenever the process goes on. Investigations of learning tell us that we learn what we want to learn, that is, we learn things related to something we want very much. In addition, modern learning theory attaches much importance to the contexts which surround learning. Memory is greatly facilitated by relationships between things learned and those being learned. Working with ideas, like working with physical objects, involves noticing or finding relationships. Any significant learning involving large quantities of facts or concepts involves the ability to make and hold together a multitude of relationships. Learning, then, must have relevance, relatedness, or it often will not take place.

Faculty members should be the first to admit this. The scholar, particularly within the kind of specialized scholarship that characterizes university work, succeeds in some measure to the extent he shuts out learning for its own sake and acquires specific knowledge related to a task at hand. Scholarly investigations proceed under a directing intelligence as well as by intuition and luck. The investigator deliberately shuts out, for a time, things which he thinks are not relevant. He specifically seeks relevant facts, related phenomena. What he puts together is a tight construct in which the parts, whether they be mathematical constructs, critical precepts, or historical facts, fit together. What is intuition or luck oftentimes if not a sense of relatedness, stumbling upon the missing

77

piece of evidence which binds together all the other particulars? If the scholarly work is of a high order, it is probably highly relevant to other investigations, to other related phenomena, to a variety of things the work was assumed not to be related to, and even to large and important matters involving individual and social well-being or survival.

What, then, do professors find so irritating in the students' desire for relevance? The irritation, I think, is not unlike that which orderly, disciplined minds feel when confronted by students who ramble on about the interrelatedness of all things. The nature of training in a discipline is to separate certain realms of knowledge. A language develops along with a methodology and a body of basic materials which define relevance as that which takes place within these confines. Any endeavor which consumes human attention has a satisfying network of internal relationships. All academic specialties, through an abundance of fact, phenomena and time and space contexts, provide these complex and varied relationships. To many faculty members, the threat inherent in the students' demands for relevance is that of being torn away from relationships that are familiar, satisfying, and still incompletely explored. The threatened faculty member does not deny that relevance is a central concept of learning but he feels that his boundaries of relevance are threatened by an expansion in which his field of relevance—call it his academic specialization—will no longer loom large or important. In the larger context, he will not be able to operate with confidence and competence.

Students, on the other hand, have many worlds to attract them and a big world of which they are just becoming a real part. How can they be expected to give up their notions of relevance, simple and unexamined as these notions may be, and accept without struggle involvement in the limited relationships which are a professor's academic concern? Having just broken away from their families, students are not prime prospects for other familial organizations. They are, in fact, attracted by notions of the whole kingdom of learning and they chafe at instruction which attempts to make at least one or two things perfectly clear. They demand relevance on their own terms, relatedness among things which matter to them.

No teacher, at any time in history, should expect otherwise. The teacher's task is to enlarge the range of relationships for the learner. Idealizing the teacher's role, we can say he opens students' eyes and makes them see. This idealization implies that, through learning, the multiplicity of the world is not only expanded but the students' capacity to deal with that multiplicity is enlarged. Somewhere in the plenitude itself, in the relationships discerned and to be discerned, and in the process of selection and evaluating that brings order to multiplicity, truth may lie.

Let us shift to less abstract considerations and examine what students mean when they say teachers and courses are not relevant. Customarily such a statement seems to mean that students cannot understand what the teacher is talking about or what possible use the course materials could have. Both statements are understandably irritating to the professor who understands his subject well enough and whose devotion makes the subject relevant for him. Students have justification for distrusting scholarship. For the multitude of scholars, any scholarship is relevant as long as it satisfies the individual scholar's specialized interest. It is surprising that professors who accept that definition are hostile to including in the curriculum the many matters—astrology, fortune-telling, tie-dyeing, beadcraft— that meet individual students' specialized interests and which create group interests not unlike those of professional societies.

Things the students know and particularly things they know well are seldom what the professors know. Nor are things once learned always available thereafter. A teacher would be wise and less often aggrieved if he adopted two fundamental teaching precepts: that a student has never learned much before; and that he will never grasp the whole of anything. Beginning there, the teacher wastes less of his vital juices berating the failure of previous teachers or the failure of his own previous teachings. More important, he expends intelligence and imagination in trying to establish relationships between what he is trying to teach and whatever the students know and value. Other things being equal, the higher the relevance for the student, the more effective the teaching.

But what of those large portions of the college curriculum which are dismissed as irrelevant? Teachers of historical subjects hear often enough how students shun everything that happened before 1930, or 1940, or 1965. Even faculty members blame the difficulties of teaching certain subjects on lack of relevance as compared with other subjects. Like most fondly-held academic notions, these contain some truth. Consider the first charge: that students find only modern studies relevant. I think it is probably true that a sense of history develops late and with some difficulty. History in the personal sense takes on significance only after the individual has accumulated some meaningful and diverse experiences. Family and environment can, to a degree, substitute for personal experience but ultimately the study of history becomes consuming because it has relevance to what the individual has experienced and is experiencing. A sense of history is difficult to establish because of the basic difficulties in holding enough in one's head at any one time to establish relationships which will give any specific moment in time relevance to what has gone before. The difficulty of making any portion of the past relevant has to be acknowledged. Since the immediate present occupies such a tiny speck in the totality of experience, however, almost every teacher who deals with any subject that cannot be contained within the hour faces a common problem. There is simply no good defense for the teacher who says, "Relevance be damned. I teach my period."

Apart from the difficulties faced by individual teachers, professors worry that student emphasis upon relevance will have a narrowing effect upon curricula. Teachers fear that priceless parts of the tradition might be lost, important but very specialized fields discarded, immediate and ephemeral considerations might rule over most of our choices. When I consider the nature of university organization and its powers of resistance, I see no real danger. Student demands for relevance would have to shut down universities from coast to coast. Even then the negotiations that restored the curriculum would soon arrive at the unweeded garden we have now. I think the academic community should listen carefully to student complaints about the relevance of curricula and to students' specific suggestions for improvement. Curricula could probably benefit from pruning in every college and university in the country.

But simply adding or subtracting from the curriculum makes little sense. The Scranton report, calling attention to student dissatisfaction with the curriculum, sounds unfortunately like a university curriculum committee: "In the search for greater relevance, subjects that are esoteric, traditional, or highly abstract, should not be neglected or eliminated, but there must also be course offerings which focus directly and concretely upon the contemporary world."[8] I do not think that statement deals with the students' main point. The curriculum is a disciplinary notion almost entirely controlled by ideas of relevance within the disciplines. Inevitably a large number of courses are included as the result of tradition and accretion. Curricula lay great stress on sequence and coverage and fairly little stress on relative value within the discipline or within the university. Curricula tend to fall into the patterns set by disciplines whether the patterns are appropriate or not. Increasingly in the past twenty years curricula have been shaped around the training of students who will go on to graduate school and attach themselves in some way to a discipline.

In all these ways, curricula can rightly be charged with not being relevant. Tradition and accretion do not necessarily give vitality to studies. Sequence and coverage are respectable ideas but sequence is not nearly so necessary as academic practice would make it seem and coverage is a frustrating illusion. Both concepts make bad teachers out of intelligent young men and women until they gain enough confidence and wisdom to realize how limiting these concepts are. Relevance, if it were not such an inflammatory word, might be a standard by which to conduct an honest examination of the curriculum. Departmental structures make the curriculum almost invulnerable in this respect. The voices of students are needed to ask blunt questions such as, "What am I supposed to get out of this course?" For anyone who takes a moment's thought about a student's education (not merely his training in a major field), the bits and pieces of the curriculum have little relationship, little relevance, to any integrated experience.

[8] Scranton Report, p. 22.

On the whole, I think students are justified in asking for relevant teaching. Effective teachers always establish relevance in one way or another. The ability to do so is not strictly dependent on the subject matter or the age of the professor, but has most to do with taking teaching seriously. Teachers must recognize that students often are not in the teacher's orbit, and that the worth and relevance of a subject do not disclose themselves in the course packaging. Finding and helping the students establish relationships between academic learning and things which matter to them is the very essence of teaching. The position of teacher is not easy to occupy in a society seemingly bent on instant obsolescence. But so far students continue to show up and are capable of being reached in any subject by any teacher with a proper respect for relevance.

Relevance confronts higher education in another disturbing way in the students' push to make colleges and universities more relevant to the outside world. The Columbia riots of 1968 offer a paradigm of the university in American society comparable to the role of American society in the world at large. The overriding issue at Columbia was the university's relationship to the community it occupied. There, as elsewhere, a multitude of important decisions had to be made about the institution's involvement and detachment from society. Without trying to assess the total effects of student riots, one can firmly say that riots and related events have drawn the college and university into the world. "American universities," the Scranton commission reported, "have special—and sometimes neglected—responsibilities to the communities in which they are located."[9] Student demands for academic programs relevant to the community cannot be set aside. The fact that universities assemble trained intelligence and gather together great stores of knowledge makes it unavoidable that some of that intelligence and knowledge should be pressed into immediate service. Not all scholars can or should have an active academic relationship with the community. The point of upholding teaching and learning as central purposes of the university is that those activities foster the detachment necessary to inquiry and the engagement that puts learning to use. The students furnish the necessary point of contact with the outside

[9] *Ibid.*, p. 21.

82

world. Through them and with them, the university's values, knowledge, expertise, and wisdom are translated into public policies. It is not merely wrongheaded to deny student demands for relevance in this broader sense. It is against the well-being of the university and society. Academic men and women are not the only ones who wall themselves off; the majority of human beings deny the relevance of a host of matters which do not touch them directly. The ineradicable presence of poverty, violence, racism, war, and human misery attests to that fact.

A second thing students seem to want is participation in important decisions affecting university policies and practices. This demand cannot help but be vexing to the faculty. It comes at a time when the faculty itself has just begun to play a large part in the important decisions of many colleges and universities. Nevertheless, faculty members should be thankful for student zeal. Apathy is still a greater deterrent to learning than excessive involvement.

The students' demands have been both political and academic. At the point of confrontation, students have demanded a voice in certain policies, such as those governing housing rules, minority programs, and allocation of resources. Occasionally they have moved into the faculty's domain by asking for substantial participation in decisions on appointing and retaining faculty. Many universities have responded to general student unrest by allowing representation of students on faculty senates or committees. At some colleges and universities, disillusion is already setting in over lack of attendance and interest in the committee assignments students have won. There is, to me, nothing disturbing in this.

The university structure, as students have charged, is authoritarian. This authoritarianism is expressed in the mechanical structures of registration, grading and certification, and in teaching. The general posture of teachers up front and students out there has been around us so long we forget what it clearly implies. Neither Socrates nor Aristotle operated that way and neither the book nor television exercises the same kind of coercive power.

Teachers should not be distressed at students who seem to want to strip them of their lecterns. Unlike mechanical structures, teachers can talk with the students. In doing so, they have a chance to establish the bond of confidence which permits one kind of authority—based on the teacher's knowledge or skill—while maintaining equality of respect. Students are sensitive to those who confuse authority of position with superiority of person. The framework of higher education gives support to both postures.

If relaxing the authoritarian manner encourages students to become involved in learning, that is all to the good. The worst thing threatened by students' inclusion on committees dealing with academic matters is that they might support conservative members of the faculty. More dangerous to what students hope to gain by inclusion in governing structures is the difficulty of sustaining participation. Student rating of faculty members as teachers, regarded by some as a usurpation of authority, does not easily gain and hold student interest. Like other forms of student participation in academic matters, student evaluation will have to be encouraged by the faculty if it is to yield sustained results. In time, at individual colleges at least, students may reach a level of participation somewhere between eagerly exercising new powers and dutifully carrying out assignments.

The only new aspect of student desires to have a say about running the university is the nature of their demands and the university's and the public's response. If we look back to a period as recent as that following the end of World War II, we can find many examples of student demands for a voice in how things were running. Returning veterans, who were dominant in the student body during that period, had the inestimable advantage of public support and the cooperation of the universities. Many of the things students are now asking for were freely given then. For example, I entered the University of Iowa in November as others were entering at the first of each month. Academic credits for outside experience were generously provided. Courses were adapted to fit shorter periods of time. The three-year B.A. degree, being advocated today, was a reality for many veterans then. Teachers in all subjects were under strong pressure to be relevant. Authority took a fair beating during that period, though experience in dealing with military bureaucracy made strategic noncompliance a more favored mode of response than defiance and confrontation.

What Students Want

The differences today are not so much in the students' demands as in the sociological conditions which at that time supported the cession of institutional power to the satisfaction of both sides. This relinquishment was accomplished without manifestoes, restructuring of governing structures, or traumatic experiences. But the conditions that permitted it are not easily reproduced, and conditions of another kind influence the nature and expression of student desires today and the faculty's response to these desires. The national publicity given to sit-ins, building takeovers, demonstrations, and incidents of violence strengthen the process through which almost any kind of conspicuous activity on a few campuses gets taken up by many. This publicity also makes the wider audience forget the general lack of student involvement.

But students can and do speak with the voice of reason as well as the voice of protest. At the project's final conference, the group which discussed student participation in shaping educational practices made the following recommendations:

> Student needs can be best met if institutional policies: (1) Encourage students to actively participate in matters affecting instructional practices. It is essential that students be given legitimate, meaningful representation on key department, college and university decision-making committees, particularly when those committees assist in determining the quality and type of education available to the students. (2) Encourage inclusion of students representing a range of age and experience. Institutional policies must not penalize students whose schedules of study do not allow them to pursue a conventional academic program. (3) Encourage students to consider interrupting their course of study if experiences beyond the campus would seem most productive of growth and development. (4) Encourage students to engage in work-study options when such action would appear to promote progress toward learning goals. In many cases this may require a re-examination of what constitutes appropriate academic activities and will necessitate the creation of more effective relationships between higher education institutions and the larger community.
>
> While it is acknowledged that there are a variety of ways in which the developmental needs of students can be met, faculty members must imaginatively evolve instructional approaches

which are engaging and meaningful to a wide range of students. It is therefore essential that college and university faculty members support in a variety of ways student decisions about which learning goals to pursue, which methods to employ in reaching these goals, and which procedures can be most effectively used to assess progress toward the goals.

The third kind of student demand presses for acknowledgment of what I will call "natural youthful inclinations." Whitehead's discussion of the "rhythm of these natural cravings of the human intelligence" helps explain my intent:

> My main position is that the dominant note of education at its beginning and at its end is freedom, but that there is an intermediate stage of discipline with freedom in subordination. Furthermore, that there is not one unique threefold cycle of freedom, discipline, and freedom; but that all mental development is composed of such cycles, and of cycles of such cycles. Such a cycle is a unit cell, or brick; and the complete stage of growth is an organic structure of such cells. In analysing any one such cell, I call the first period of freedom the "stage of Romance," the intermediate period of discipline I call the "stage of Precision," and the final period of freedom is the "stage of Generalization." . . . In no part of education can you do without discipline or can you do without freedom; but in the stage of romance the emphasis must always be on freedom.[10]

Many manifestations of the "youth culture" are romantic manifestations and college students cannot help being affected by this emphasis. There is nothing very new or sinister in this. *Werther* was not written in our time; Mozart was as young and prolific a composer as John Lennon or Paul McCartney; Thoreau was growing beans in the 1840s and writing, "I have lived some thirty years on this planet, and I have yet to hear the first syllable of valuable or even earnest advice from my seniors." Despite the fact that "romanticism" is a firm part of the college curriculum, many people associated with higher education remain suspicious of it. Learning is chiefly and unfortunately concerned with mastering facts. As Whitehead wrote: "There is no comprehension apart from ro-

[10] *The Aims of Education,* pp. 42, 44.

mance. It is my strong belief that the cause of so much failure in the past has been due to the lack of careful study of the due place of romance. Without the adventure of romance, at the best you get inert knowledge without initiative, and at the worst you get contempt of ideas—without knowledge."[11] There are rich possibilities for learning in the romantic outlook of many students today. Although this outlook often seems to appear in fairly freaky forms, most of these forms can be regarded as the expression of natural youthful inclinations. One should not minimize the serious pressures upon students and the serious nature of their protests but students have always had surplus energies to expend, sometimes in destructive ways. Frederick Rudolph, in *The American College and University*, says of the student riots in at least fifteen colleges between 1800 and 1875, "The rebellions documented the failure of the colleges to provide altogether suitable 'rites of adolescence,' satisfactory outlets for quite normal animal energy and human imagination."[12]

It is important to recognize the need for students to burst out, to exert their freedom. It is not enough to cite the permissiveness of our society and to blame such permissiveness for the further liberties students take. Adolescents always achieve important freedoms regardless of when permissiveness began. And parents, home, and school are there, regardless of how little restraint they seem to impose. The driving force of sex holds adolescents in another kind of captivity. At age 16, a driver's license opens up a host of freedoms. At 18, males become eligible for the draft, and all citizens become eligible to vote. It is more important than ever that we move "to restore the student to his rightful place at the center of the college's activities."[13]

We do students an injustice and probably violate our own sense of the learning process if we give up on discipline in exasperation over the demands by some students for what seems like complete freedom. The unstructured learning experience some students

[11] *Ibid.*, p. 44.
[12] New York: Alfred A. Knopf, 1962, p. 98.
[13] N. Sanford, *Where Colleges Fail* (San Francisco: Jossey-Bass, 1967), p. xiv.

seem to crave as often as not turns out to be a learning experience with a different structure. In general, I think the faculty's view is more flawed than the students'. The faculty too easily forgets the unassertive but unavoidable structuring that molds everything in a traditional, institutional, departmentalized framework. Faculty efforts to break out of structures should be more than cautious concessions to students who have found a voice. I think we need not fear inviting the students to help teachers shape modes of instruction. Nor should we get alarmed at the erosion of required courses and degree requirements. It is not likely that absolute freedom or absolute discipline will rule over education. If we are to arrive at a workable balance today, we need to observe and respond to the rhythms of learning felt by this generation of students.

Many manifestations of youth culture can be related to the preceding discussion. Students have natural inclinations markedly different from those of professors with respect to the ideal versus the real, to sensory pleasures versus intellectual satisfactions, immediate as against deferred pleasures, rationality and irrationality, work and play, excitement and repose, even toward learning, teaching, and knowledge. The most important single fact about the youth culture may be the the rising birth rate from 1945 to 1961 and the decline thereafter. It was the increasing numbers of young people which gave basic support to the youth culture. From 1958 on, these marked increases began to affect 12-year-olds, and by 1966, the 12- to 20-year-old group was dominant. I do not intend to argue that this trend alone explains the ideas and actions that have been current for the last ten years. We should, however, remember that many of the phenomena that seem upsetting, even threatening, are manifestations of youth at any period. These phenomena are magnified by numbers, by the possibilities of commercial exploitation, and by the color they create for news and entertainment media.

Consequential shifts in attitudes and values are likely to come about in a democracy through sheer force of numbers. Within higher education, the presence of even a small minority whose absolute size is large can bring about many shifts. Whether or not the youth culture has achieved a revolution in attitudes and values, it has certainly confronted the collegiate and general culture with various versions of different life styles. The youthful embodiments of these life styles are seen everywhere. The body of beliefs many students share seem to emphasize brotherhood, feeling, joy, mysticism, ritual, being, and body and spirit more than mind. These beliefs all flow from natural youthful inclinations which formal educational structures tend to repress. Colleges and universities would do well to respond to these general promptings.

Brotherhood, for example, can hardly be considered a bad idea. Student pressures for a less competitive, more cooperative learning environment seem worth supporting. The grading system is improving under pressures from students to get away from the worst effects of the system. The need to widen educational opportunities and to recognize the worth of all individuals by some measure other than academic attainment is surely chronic. Pressures from racial minorities must become pressures from the dominant majority to move brotherhood closer to reality. The connection between war and man's competitive, antagonistic strivings cannot be denied.

The emphasis on feeling, although it supports transient fads and enduring irrationality, is again a necessary corrective to an often desiccated intellectualism in higher education. Universities could well afford to more actively pursue joy in scholarship. "Undoubtedly," Whitehead writes, "pain is one subordinate means of arousing an organism to action. But it only supervenes on the failure of pleasure. Joy is the normal healthy spur for the *élan vital*."[14]

The current emphasis upon being, experience, and identity may be irritating because of the way students seem preoccupied with the present, with the self, and with sensory gratifications. But youth is always a time for developing a sense of what one is and might be. Colleges fail dismally when they do not contribute wisely to that development. Teachers have a great responsibility to foster this self-exploration. We should not be fooled into thinking students have no broader visions simply because they seem so caught up in the moment. Whitehead says one vital aim of education is "the development of character along a path of natural activity, in itself plea-

[14] *The Aims of Education*, p. 42.

surable. The subordinate stiffening of discipline must be directed to secure some long-time good; although an adequate object must not be too far below the horizon if the necessary interest is to be retained."[15] Many of the students I have encountered want something to do. They want their talents to be put to use. This desire, as it translates itself into demands for change in the academic program, seeks more credit for outside experience, more relationships between academic experience and the outside world. Four-year colleges and universities have largely neglected the work their graduates might do unless that work involves continuing in the university. A closer relationship with the junior colleges might be a healthy corrective to a faculty view that seldom focuses on what the students might actually do while they are in college and when they get out.

Most disturbing about the values of students identified with the youth culture are the implied demands these values make upon professors. At the heart of that most persistent student complaint—that professors do not care—is a desire for professors to be more than academic competence inclines them to be. To some degree, students have been sold on the examples of great men whose spirits hover over both students and faculty and whose living counterparts should be walking among them. The faculty is being called upon to evoke and embody these spirits. The specific demand may be for the teacher who can draw out the learner's own sense of who he is, help dignify it, enlarge it, and keep before him the possibilities of who he might be. In that sense of self is what Benjamin DeMott calls, "the variousness and fullness of life." If this aspiration seems to exert greater power over students today, it may be because the glimpses of fulfillment dangle so enticingly before everyone. It is to the students' credit, I think, that the desires of a recognizable part of the student body today are not nearly as materialistic or hedonistic as they well might be. The main reason for listening to what students seem to want is not to find out what to give them, but to move both teachers and students to realize what higher learning might give us all.

[15] *Ibid.*, p. 42.

CHAPTER 6

Learning to Teach

The processes by which young people become college teachers seldom fit a purposeful design. College teaching rarely appears as a career possibility before a student reaches college. Even then the decision to become a college teacher is usually made late and is strongly influenced by drift rather than by planning. Preparation in graduate school is only indirectly concerned with teaching, and the job market for academic positions is almost as difficult to describe as the processes by which applicants eventually come into the job market. It is not surprising that most disciplines were unprepared for a sudden surplus of Ph.D. candidates. In the sixties, graduate students appeared almost everywhere in sufficient numbers to permit departments to be selective and jobs, especially the large number created within higher education itself, always seemed to be available.

No great blame need be directed at departments or institutions for failing to anticipate a change in the market. Long range planning is a comparatively recent development in institutional management. Even with long range planning, departments tend to leave the details of supply and demand to the central administration.

The hindsight of angry graduate students referring to the surplus as a "glut of Ph.D.s" makes it appear that the change should have been anticipated. But projections, which are not always accurate, disagreed widely. The present condition may cause the profession to give more attention to identifying college teaching talent, to preparation of college teachers in the graduate schools, and to their placement in colleges and universities.

Rather than summarize various statistical studies of the nature of young people entering the profession and the ways they enter, the following paragraphs will sketch one reasonably typical picture of a student on his way to becoming a college teacher. Such a student is likely to be male, to come from parents with a college background or even from a teaching family. Both parents have college degrees, and his father's occupation is probably white collar, clerical, managerial, or professional. The candidate will have earned good grades in high school and in his undergraduate work. His teachers in public school probably encouraged him to go on to college. He may have been a member of an honors society or have received some other recognition of academic excellence.

Typically, his major gave him no direct access to a job and his good academic record made him consider going on to graduate school in his senior year. Unlike the academically talented woman student, he probably did not take the courses in education necessary to make public school teaching a possibility. In any event, graduate school was attractive to him because many of his friends were going on. The draft also played a part in his decision to stay in school. Not quite strong enough a student to receive a Woodrow Wilson fellowship, and a little afraid of entrance requirements at the top graduate schools, he decided to apply for an assistantship at a number of state universities. When he received two firm offers, he accepted one from the more prestigious school and began his graduate work the fall after receiving his B.A. degree.

After two years as an assistant, with his Master's degree almost completed, he decides to stay on and go for the Ph.D. He might be able to get a job outside or teach in a junior college with an M.A., but a couple of faculty members have encouraged him to get a Ph.D. Academic life is congenial and though he has some regrets about giving up some earlier notions about going into one of the professional schools, he may not do badly in college teaching. Since he now has a wife (another graduate student), he has some problems seeing clearly ahead to the Ph.D., but she is willing to work full-time in the registrar's office and she wants him to go on. If he can just wind up the M.A. thesis this summer. . . .

One can add to the above description whatever individual experience indicates should be added. Certainly, the kinds of people involved and the patterns of their preparation are not as unvaried as a composite picture implies. College teachers emerge from quite unacademic families and out of long sustained desires and some are young women who do not let marriage break into their careers. Nor is the preceding description intended to reflect upon the individual or the process. Those who find themselves in college teaching express satisfaction with their choice. Forty-four per cent of the faculty in Ruth Eckert's samples indicated they were "very satisfied," while another 39 per cent said they were "satisfied" with their choice of career. In fact, 85 per cent said they would again choose an academic career if they had a chance to.[1] This composite sketch is intended to provide a background for discussion of the ways in which individuals are identified and encouraged to enter the profession.

It seems obvious that little early identification or encouragement actually goes on. There is indirect encouragement of bright students by public school teachers who want such students to go on to college and through identification with high school and college teachers who view the students' accomplishments favorably and who take an interest in their development. These may amount to an effectively operating selection system instrumental to the high degree of satisfaction professors later express toward their careers.

Casual acquaintance in public school and college with teaching as a profession is inaccurate but influential in various important ways. Perhaps the most obvious distortion is the predominantly feminine presence in the lower schools and predominantly masculine or feminine teachers of certain subjects in the high schools and colleges.

[1] R. Eckert, H. Y. Williams, D. H. Anderson, *The University of Minnesota Faculty: Who Serves and Why?* (Minneapolis: University of Minnesota, 1970), pp. 16–19.

Through such general conditions, favorable and unfavorable impressions of teachers and teaching may be created. Discouragement of the unacademic and encouragement of the bookish seem to be part of the general impact of public schools. A narrowing of the range of possible students who might eventually enter college teaching may be the result of impressions casually established in the public schools and in college.

Though college teaching is certainly a career possibility that should be carefully identified and made known to high school students, it probably is not very forcefully brought to their attention. Students in high school are probably like the student who said to me, "When you think of teaching in high school, it's always twelfth grade or below. You think you'd never be qualified for teaching in a college." In college, teaching becomes a distinct possibility. Much could be done there to identify prospective college teachers and to make the full dimensions of college teaching more visible to them.

The chances are very high that a student becomes interested in college teaching because he likes college life and college pursuits and has had a college teacher with whom he identifies. It has already been pointed out that departmental structures and discipline-oriented professors tend to mold undergraduate majors inclined to favor the student bound for graduate school and to a career somewhat like that of his professors. In some fields, particularly in the sciences and engineering, where attractive nonacademic positions are available, students may not necessarily be drawn into teaching. And if they are, the expectation of continuing research may have a strong influence on career choice. In many fields, such as English, history, and philosophy, where there are few positions for practitioners, a decision to go on with graduate work is, whether the person is aware of it or not, a decision for college or university teaching.

What seems most obvious about this process and least favorable to attempts at increasing the emphasis given to teaching or at altering traditional patterns is the fact that the student who is like a majority of his professors, who finds the departmental major congenial, and who accepts the routines of preparation, step by step, has the greatest chance of becoming a college teacher. It is probably fortunate that the decision is made late. Otherwise the chances of exactly duplicating the models future professors have before them would probably be higher. As it is, the decision is as often a final capitulation to undesirable aspects of the process as it is a joyful decision to concentrate energies on the task ahead. Surely it is not satisfactory to have an identification process within the collegiate structure which tends to select those who conform to existing patterns and to subject them to a long educational and acculturation process which heightens the conforming effects of the selection process.

Formal counseling can help widen the range of possibilities for students and increase the diversity of those who might profitably be drawn into teaching careers. Counseling is one aspect of education which has suffered amidst the general neglect of the undergraduate program. Career counseling in most academic departments has been all but nonexistent in the large, graduate-oriented universities and not much more evident in the colleges. Informal counseling suffers everywhere by virtue of the simple fact that faculty members know so little about opportunities outside the academic world.

The larger aspects of counseling are not my concern. Academic men and women know something about college and university teaching and their knowledge could be put to use in direct, informational ways that could supplement the informal and partial view students otherwise get. It should be possible for departments to do a number of potentially worthwhile things in the identification of talented college teachers. What the department does is probably more crucial than what is done in formal counseling outside the department. Specifically, the department could identify the multiple characteristics important for the college teacher, and these identified characteristics could become a force in shaping the graduate program and in selecting students for that program. The department could afford its majors various teaching or teaching-related opportunities useful to prospective public school and college teachers. The department could specifically use the involvement of students in evaluation of teachers, in examination of curricula, and in the general policies and practices of the department to increase student interest in college teaching as a career and to add to their understanding of it. The department could become involved in education, in the preparation of college teachers, and not leave all specific aspects of informing and preparing to chance.

The process of admitting students to graduate work is about as indirectly related to future teaching careers as is the general inclination of public school teachers to encourage bright students to go on to college. There is one difference. The student's vision has often been narrowed down from the time he enters college to the time he enters graduate school to work in a single discipline. Success in this discipline, his undergraduate major, rules the policies of admission.

The student must have achieved a high grade point average, preferably in all subjects but certainly in his major. He needs to have received high scores on a departmental comprehensive exam or on the Graduate Record Examination. He may be asked to submit letters of recommendation which tend to reinforce the statistical information about his intelligence and which strongly stress his ability to do the research work required of the Ph.D. The student's potential as a teacher is seldom questioned and specific questions which might bear upon teaching competence—breadth as well as depth, lively curiosity, desire to work with students, ability to synthesize and clarify, command of verbal communication, diversity of interests—are lightly regarded if they are asked about at all.

The trouble with graduate admission procedures as they exist is that when they are rigorously applied, when a high level of cognitive competence is required, these procedures exclude many potentially gifted teachers and still include many whose qualities of mind, emotion, and experience are not favorable to teaching. When admissions policies are relaxed, as they are when large numbers of graduate assistants are needed, the numbers of variously-gifted teachers may increase but so do the numbers of those unsuited to teaching and weak in scholarship. Admissions policies and procedures favorable for teaching would not depend so heavily upon grades and test achievements; would not be so strictly confined to previous accomplishments in a discipline and assume further intensified study in that discipline; would use personality inventories and other means to assess aptitude for teaching; and would include, at the Ph.D. level, a personal interview before a panel representative

96

not only of the department's scholarly interest but of the department's and the university's interest in teaching.

The procedures for admission to Ph.D. programs are less than they should be if the academic community really set great store by the Ph.D. degree. Even the most demanding graduate schools do not characteristically give candidates the benefit of a searching personal interview before a departmental board. In the past decade, numbers have provided an easy excuse for avoiding such time-consuming processes. Anyway, the unfit are rejected, not so much along the way as at the eleventh hour by the oral or comprehensive exam. This is an odd way to run a rational enterprise supposedly at the highest level of rationality. With the tightening of admissions to Ph.D. programs, institutions can afford to adopt more personal, revealing procedures. Personal attention to the candidate, involving an inquiry into where he thinks he is going, what he wants to do, and the kind of equipment he seems to possess for doing it, would help us to identify and encourage effective college teachers.

Inadequate admissions procedures for graduate schools and degree programs might be defensible if more attention were given to students' progress after they were admitted. But a candidate seldom has to face the important questions of where he is in his progress, not just toward a degree, but toward a future career. Instead, he is given obstacles to hurdle by which he can measure his own progress: the language exams with a roomful of candidates and a written notification of success or failure, crucial course examinations graded in due time with marks recorded, degree examinations basing their verdicts on limited measures of a narrow range of intellectual competence and casting vague doubts or giving vague support to everything else. Part of the high cost of graduate education stems from the reduced numbers of students and the supposedly greater degree of personal involvement of the faculty with each one. It is only reasonable that advanced degree candidates meet periodically with members of the graduate faculty not to discuss the thesis or to take an examination but to assess their development as prospective college and university teachers.

If selection procedures for college teachers are lacking, and admissions procedures to degree programs are inadequate, what of the preparation programs for the college teacher? It is hard to choose among the critics of existing programs and difficult to find reasoned, impassioned defenders of what exists. Criticism has a long history, almost as long as the existence of the Ph.D. degree in America. Perhaps the most fitting place to begin is with William James' "The Ph.D. Octopus." It describes the general condition as accurately today as it did when it was written:

> Our higher degrees were instituted for the laudable purpose of stimulating scholarship, especially in the form of "original research." Experience has proved that great as the love of truth may be among men, it can be made still greater by adventitious rewards. The winning of a diploma certifying mastery and marking a barrier successfully passed, acts as a challenge to the ambitious; and if the diploma will help to gain bread-winning positions also, its power as a stimulus to work is tremendously increased. So far, we are on innocent ground; it is well for a country to have research in abundance, and our graduate schools do but apply a normal psychological spur. But the institutionizing on a large scale of any natural combination of need and motive always tends to run into technicality and to develop a tyrannical Machine with unforeseen powers of exclusion and corruption. . . . To interfere with the free development of talent, to obstruct the natural play of supply and demand in the teaching profession, to foster academic snobbery by the prestige of certain privileged institutions, to transfer accredited value from essential manhood to an outward badge, to blight hopes and promote invidious sentiments, to divert the attention of aspiring youth from direct dealings with truth to the passing of examinations—such consequences, if they exist, ought surely to be regarded as drawbacks to the system, and an enlightened public consciousness ought to be keenly alive to the importance of reducing their amount. Candidates themselves do seem to be keenly conscious of some of these evils, but outside of their ranks or in the general public no such consciousness, so far as I can see, exists; or if it does exist, it fails to express itself aloud. Schools, Colleges, and Universities, appear enthusiastic over the entire system, just as it stands, and unanimously applaud all its developments.[2]

[2] *Memories and Studies* (Longmans, Green, and Co., 1917), pp. 334–337.

Learning to Teach

The most recent and thorough examination of graduate school practices is Ann Heiss's *Challenges to Graduate Schools,* a study of Ph.D. programs in ten major universities and review of the major literature on graduate education.[3] Heiss, in her concluding chapter, acknowledges most of the accepted characteristics of graduate work in a modern university. These emphasize the primacy of research and the dependence of research on external sources for support among the Heiss recommendations, these are directly relevant to the subject of this chapter:

> Although the paramount interest of the graduate department is the production of specialists for the discipline, it should not permit the academic program or the process to become dehumanized in the interest of developing the discipline. . . . In commenting on their educational experiences students frequently described them as "dehumanized in the interest of scientism." This criticism was pervasive throughout the twelve disciplines in the study.

> Teaching should be reinstated as a primary purpose and responsibility of the university.

> In response to the criticism leveled against college and university teaching, and in view of the radical changes in teaching strategies and technology, the graduate school should reaffirm its responsibility as the teacher of teachers by offering carefully designed programs of teacher preparation for doctoral students who plan to enter academic careers.

> Graduate schools should give serious consideration to the need for a new degree for college teaching such as the Doctor of Arts or the doctorate in a substantive field. The use of a single degree program to certify the preparation of researchers, teachers, leaders in government, business, industry, and many other careers has been criticized for decades as unrealistic. . . . Most of the criticisms of the Ph.D. center on the charge that the program emphasizes research preparation and neglects preparation for teaching.[4]

The project's booklet *Career Development of the Effective*

[3] San Francisco: Jossey-Bass, 1970.
[4] *Ibid.,* pp. 270–302.

99

College Teacher[5] deals extensively with the subject of preparing college teachers in the graduate school. Individual disciplinary associations have shown an active interest in the subject and the Council of Graduate Schools itself has been examining the possibilities of a Doctor of Arts degree. Since the sciences set the pattern so much for advanced degree work, it is important to consider the criticisms made within scientific disciplines. Eight commissions on undergraduate programs in the sciences established through the disciplinary associations and supported by the National Science Foundation have all expressed concern for the ways in which graduate programs train college teachers.

> It should be understood that no academic program or degree in itself qualifies an individual to teach effectively at any level unless this preparation is accompanied by a genuine interest in teaching and by professional activities reflecting continuing mathematical growth.[6]

> There is a strong need to turn a much larger percentage of the creative effort of the entire profession to the task of understanding what we are trying to do in instruction, and how we may do it better.[7]

> The university is the only place where future teachers in universities and in colleges of all types can learn to teach undergraduates. If the job is not done by the universities, it is not done.[8]

A booklet recently published by the Commission in the Biological Sciences offers sound advice for all graduate disciplines. The commission relates the inadequacy of Ph.D. programs as preparation for college teaching to these factors: teaching has a lower status than research; subject matter training is thought to be all that is

---

[5] K. Eble (Washington, D.C.: American Association of University Professors and Association of American Colleges, 1971).

[6] Commission on the Undergraduate Program in Mathematics, *Qualifications for a College Faculty in Mathematics* (Mathematical Association of America, 1967), p. 2.

[7] E. L. Jossem, "The Challenge Renewed," *American Journal of Physics,* 1968, *36*(11), 1033–1034.

[8] *Commission on Undergraduate Education in the Biological Sciences News,* 1969, *6*(2), p. 3.

necessary for the training of college teachers; the schedule is too crowded and the faculty too busy to give attention to teaching; *education* is a pejorative term in academia; and strong conflicts exist as to whether and how teachers can be taught.

Among the commission's recommendations for improving such preparation are that graduate departments consider offering the D.A. or other practitioner's degree; allow creative investigations of the teaching of biology to be used as dissertations; improve programs for teaching assistants; consider developing seminars or courses on effective teaching as a companion to the teaching experience; and find ways to enlist the participation of senior memers of the department in improvement of the program for future teachers.[9]

After examining movements toward reform in many disciplines and discussing this subject at the various conferences, I would suggest the following guidelines for the development of better programs of preparation for college teachers.

First, consequential attention within the department to the graduate student's development as teacher. This might include: involvement of senior staff in lower-division, nonmajor courses; team teaching in which senior and junior staff members and graduate students are involved; direct involvement of senior staff in formal and informal programs of supervision of teacher training for graduate fellows or assistants; departmental efforts to establish an interest in education—lower school and higher—and in teaching among staff and graduate students.

Second, enlightened experience in teaching. This would entail: involvement of the entire staff in working with graduate students as teachers; recognition of teaching experience as an integral part of the program for advanced degree candidates who envision college or university teaching as a future career; general reduction in the class hours taught by teaching assistants; provisions for graduate assistants or fellows to teach a variety of courses including

[9] D. Dean, *Preservice Preparation of College Biology Teachers* (Washington, D.C.: Commission on Undergraduate Education in the Biological Sciences, 1970), pp. 1–13.

courses related to academic programs; provisions for teaching in contexts other than the university.

Third, inclusion within graduate programs of formal and informal studies of teaching and learning and of the broader aspects of higher education.

Fourth, broadening the dissertation option to include the preparation of courses and curricular materials and pedagogical investigations related to the discipline.

Fifth, including some form of ongoing examination of the degree candidate's developing capacities as a teacher.

Some of these guidelines are highly acceptable to graduate departments; others are not. None of them are intended to apply to the preparation of graduate students who envision research careers which are not connected with a university or which do not entail teaching. In a given department, willingness to modify programs is probably closely related to the prominence given research within the department and to the degree to which college and university teaching is the primary occupational opportunity open to those studying for Ph.D. degrees. Graduate departments in scientific disciplines have a closer identification between faculty and students, a higher degree of satisfaction on the part of the student, and a greater involvement by the faculty with the student's research than do departments in other disciplines.

An indication of how these guidelines may square with existing practices and with suggestions for change is afforded by the faculty and departmental responses to questions raised in the recent Study of Education at Stanford. In general, the responses to the twelve questions put to each school and department granting the Ph.D. degree support the conservative image of graduate schools. Strong majority responses endorsed existing practices in seven of ten questions about possible changes in the Ph.D. program. Only in response to the questions, "Should Ph.D. candidates be required to do some intensive supervised teaching as a regular part of their graduate program" and "Should the present nine-quarter residence requirement be dropped," were there substantial majorities favoring change. However, fifteen departments said Yes and thirteen said No (eleven no response) to the question: Should the route to the

Ph.D. be broadened so as to permit award of the degree to students whose primary interest is a teaching rather than a research career? To the accompanying questions which further refined this point of inquiry, five responded Yes as against eighteen No (sixteen no response) to the proposal for "establishment of a teaching degree such as the M. Phil.," while fourteen found "the present program and degree structure satisfactory" as against no negative responses and twenty-five "no response."[10]

The Stanford responses coincide with general expressions of opinions I have heard elsewhere and coincide reasonably well with specific data available with respect to graduate work in English and the biological sciences. As regards efforts at strengthening teacher preparation, there seems to be general receptivity to the idea of broadening the Ph.D. program to acknowledge (if not to specifically prepare) candidates whose major interest is teaching. Supervised teaching seems to have the endorsement of a strong majority in the profession, in major graduate schools, and in almost all disciplines. In part, this is simply an endorsement of common practices, and the reasons for endorsement mix a genuine interest in preparation of teachers with the advantages of employing graduate assistants. Further, when we examine what constitutes supervision, the involvement of faculty members is slight. Proposals to increase this involvement, which graduate students seem to favor, would probably diminish the support among graduate departments. A strong negative response to the question in the Stanford report which proposes attaching each graduate student to a faculty tutor who would assume major responsibility for "guiding and evaluating the student's progress" corroborates this supposition.

Stanford departments were also strongly opposed to amending dissertation specifications "to permit an alternative to the present research emphasis." The reply from the department of fine arts —"No, dissertations are research projects, not teaching exercises"— seems surprisingly ungenerous since one could as easily say "the fine arts are music, poetry, painting, and sculpture, not research projects." Only the Education department at Stanford favored changes

[10] The Study of Education at Stanford, *Graduate Education* (Stanford University, 1969), VII, pp. 27–35.

103

in the dissertation requirement for students preparing for college teaching. Several departments in the natural sciences expressed favor toward "alternatives such as creative synthesis or interpretation of existing materials or major design efforts." One department favored "more reasonable goals."

One can fairly read into these responses an adverse reaction to most things smacking of "education." Inclusion within graduate programs of formal and informal studies in teaching and learning and in the broader aspects of higher education would not be acceptable to many departments because of this reaction. The more such work might move toward courses in education, the less acceptable the proposal might become. However, a number of successful seminars which deal with aspects of teaching and other professional matters are being taught as part of graduate programs by faculty members from some disciplines. Graduate departments might accept such informal course work if it came under departmental or graduate school auspices.

But the guidelines set forth are not assumed to be acceptable at present to graduate departments. The present climate for change is, I think, generally favorable for strengthening some aspects of the preparation program for college teachers. In a separate survey of Ph.D. programs in English, most graduate schools sampled said they were in the midst of examining the program and anticipated changes. In the Stanford report, the two extensive published responses to the examination of graduate education were strongly critical of the conservative nature of the inquiry. One of these, a proposal by Mark Mancall, associate professor of history, includes a short survey of the development of graduate study ending with the observation: "What is most remarkable about the history of graduate education in the United States is that many of the same problems and issues have been raised decade after decade, with no real solution forthcoming."[11]

I mention Mancall's response because his proposals for the broader reform of graduate education go beyond my specific concern with teaching. Mancall focuses on the conflicts between undergraduate and graduate education somewhat as I have, and relates

[11] *Ibid.*, p. 62.

these to the conflict between the concept of knowledge for the sake of knowledge and the utilitarian uses of knowledge, and to the pre-eminence of science and the influence of science upon all other fields of graduate work. Mancall feels, "the emphasis on research training and professionalism that characterizes our graduate education raises serious questions concerning the preparation of educators for undergraduate or college level education . . . The graduate curriculum provides little or no time for broad educational experiences, which have been largely relegated to undergraduate education where, in turn, the product of the graduate curriculum executes this task but poorly."[12]

His proposal envisions both a new degree, the Master of Philosophy, equivalent to the Ph.D., and a new higher degree, Doctor of Humanities, Doctor of Social Science, or Doctor of Science, which would come in midcareer or later as a result of distinguished written research work of very high merit. The great growth in the number of Ph.D. degrees granted annually (394 in 1908, 15,000-plus today), in the number of institutions awarding them (38 in 1908, 200-plus today), and in fields in which they are awarded (149 in 1920, 550-plus today) is a good reason for taking such proposals seriously. But despite the facts that the Doctor of Arts degree is currently receiving much support and that postdoctoral research is common in the sciences, I doubt new degrees will soon gain wide acceptance.

The Doctor of Arts degree bears most directly upon the need for well prepared college teachers. The Carnegie Commission has attempted to get established universities to inaugurate such programs (Brown, University of Michigan, Claremont Center, University of Washington) and has encouraged lesser universities to opt for the D.A. instead of the Ph.D. (Idaho State, Ball State, Stephen A. Austin University). As yet the programs that have emerged bear close resemblance to existing Ph.D. programs. The endorsement of the D.A. by the Association of State Colleges and Universities may not be helpful, for one of the recognized problems with an alternate degree is to have that degree carry as much prestige as the Ph.D. Identification of the D.A. degree with institutions of middling

[12] *Ibid.*, p. 63.

stature would not enhance chances for the degree to gain respect. Under present market conditions, when advanced degree candidates are scrambling for jobs, it is difficult to persuade students to choose a new degree. The Council of Graduate Schools has shown leadership in sponsoring serious discussions of Doctor of Arts degree programs, but I do not think the Council has moved large numbers of the dominant graduate schools or the disciplines toward strong support. Nor has anyone convincingly demonstrated that undergraduate colleges would give preference to holders of the D.A. degree when employing professional staff.

The prospects for a new teaching degree do not seem very good. Perhaps it is most important that energies not get dissipated in arguments about whether to reform the Ph.D. or work toward a new degree. The educational establishment is large and varied enough and the need sufficiently urgent to justify efforts in both directions. Arthur Eastman's remarks in the *Proceedings of the Wingspread Conference on the Doctor of Arts Degree,* sponsored by the Council of Graduate Schools (Washington, D.C.) in 1970, summarize attitudes expressed there toward both the Ph.D. and the D.A. as preparation for college teaching:

> General agreement existed that undergraduate education requires a breadth of interest, a competence in teaching, a concern for students unfortunately somewhat rare today. According to the consensus, the causes lie in the failure of graduate institutions to concern themselves with the needs of their clients, a neglect that is the obverse side of their typical emphasis on research and the discovery of new knowledge. Undergraduate departments, staffed by Ph. D.'s, hire according to graduate school standards, reward according to graduate school standards, and, whatever they say about good teaching or general education, tend to think and act in the old specializing and frequently irrelevant patterns.
>
> Educationally we are a multitudinous and heterogeneous society. At present the burgeoning community colleges are more to be served with good master's programs than with doctorates. In the main, the Ph. D.-granting institutions are too chained by their traditions to gratify the undergraduate need for good, broad, interested teaching. Granted that you cannot make teachers out of nonteachers or excellent teachers out of poor ones, the D.A.

offers significant new hope. It is an effort to unfreeze the locked-in pattern of research-publication-reward that identifies departments and dominates the sociology of graduate and undergraduate education. It is an effort to make rational our educational priorities. It is more than worth the try.

Underlying present advanced degree programs in the graduate schools is the firm belief that subject matter preparation is adequate preparation for teaching. Departments have been conscientious in seeing that their standards are high, that faculty members are competent scholars, and that the degree programs treat subject matter adequately. The selection of research problems has not always been enlightened but research has been reasonably well-supervised and made to meet exacting standards. Still, course preparation fails to consider what kind of advanced education might be most desirable for a future college teacher. The guidelines I have suggested would involve changes in the various requirements that define a Ph.D. program. But substantial changes in subject matter preparation may be necessary if advanced degree programs are to produce effective college teachers. In most disciplines, needs for more breadth, more interdisciplinary work, more internal relationships among courses, and more relationship of courses to educational aims ought to influence revisions of subject matter preparation.

Supposing the Ph.D. candidate does complete his work, how does he go about finding a suitable job? The process is inexact, inefficient, and not very satisfactory for candidates or for institutions. Theodore Caplow and Reece J. McGee in *The Academic Marketplace* thoroughly analyze all aspects of job placement, recruiting, and related matters.

Like the individual, the university suffers from ignorance and poor communication in an increasingly complex situation which plainly requires knowledge and effective communication. The most salient feature of this ignorance is the inability of the department to obtain anything approaching a complete list of available candidates for vacant positions, or to determine the real availability of candidates under consideration, or to get accurate reports on current supply and demand in the disciplinary market.[13]

Though conditions in the job market have changed since the Caplow and McGee study was published, the workings of the job market have probably changed little. A decade earlier, the President's Commission on Higher Education criticized recruitment and placement practices of the profession and recommended the establishment of a nationwide clearing house of information regarding personnel needs of colleges and universities. Efforts to establish national placement procedures have produced few results. The power of departments may always stand in the way of college- and university-wide and professionwide placement efforts. But improved practices within the disciplines may be a step toward a consolidation of efforts from which a rational placement system might emerge.

[13] New York: Basic Books, 1958, p. 238.

CHAPTER 7

Faculty Development

$$\text{※}\diamond\text{※}\diamond\text{※}\diamond\text{※}\diamond\text{※}\diamond\text{※}\diamond\text{※}\diamond\text{※}\diamond\text{※}\diamond\text{※}$$

Attempts to identify and evaluate effective teaching lead naturally to efforts to develop and maintain effective teachers. The interest these activities arouse has much to do with creating a favorable environment for teaching and learning. The project's work in faculty development attempted to examine the careers of college teachers starting with training in graduate school through retirement from active teaching. The booklet *Career Development of the Effective College Teacher* discusses the subject both in terms of the stages of chronological development and of the importance of the reward system, institutional flexibility, and individual and institutional forces for leadership and change.[1]

In this chapter, I focus upon the early, middle, and late years of a college teacher. The various project conferences identified the following as important priorities for career development: (1) the need to improve the preparation of teachers in graduate schools and to make better use of the teaching assistantship; (2) the need to examine professional values and to alter the reward system so

[1] Eble, pp. 1–13, 36–95, 115–129.

that effective teaching is adequately recognized and rewarded; (3) the establishment of adequate career development systems as part of regular institutional policies and practices; (4) leadership from deans, department chairmen, and other administrative officers and faculty in supporting and encouraging teaching excellence; (5) increased flexibility in practices and structures so that ways are available to draw upon the diverse talents of faculty members and to meet changing interests, competences, and needs at various stages in the teacher's career; (6) examination of the myths and stereotypes which adversely affect teachers and teaching.

The first two priorities are treated in Chapters Six and Eight. Others will be discussed here in sufficient detail to highlight specific ideas which came under discussion within the broader topic. The need to establish adequate career development systems within institutions cannot be too strongly emphasized. But during a period of financial stringency, it is a need most likely to be set aside. The general lack of faculty development programs is evident in the responses to a questionnaire the project sent out to AAUP members. Faculty members from 142 different institutions were almost unanimous in responding negatively to the main question, "My institution (does, does not) have an effective faculty development system."

In response to the second question, "Outside of the departmental program and budget, my institution provides specific support for (research, teaching, service)," about 60 per cent of the respondents reported specific support for research. About 10 per cent reported specific support for teaching, and even fewer for service. Eighteen respondents said their institution offered no support outside of the department budgets for research, teaching, or service. The few replies which identified effective faculty development systems indicated that institutional support was provided for all three.

The project's conferences, my visits to campuses, and my discussion of the question with two very large groups of faculty from different institutions corroborate this contention. In the universities, support for research is substantial from inside and outside sources. The sabbatical leave is the most common form of general institutional support for faculty renewal. However, only about 60 per cent of institutions have such leaves, even fewer if one looks

110

closely at the restrictions placed upon the granting of sabbaticals or upon the activities deemed appropriate for such leaves. Such an obvious and important practice as setting aside a portion of the budget for faculty development is rare.

We are left with a variety of practices of lesser significance: financial assistance for attendance at professional meetings; conferences, or workshops, or visiting lecturers, or consultants on teaching; load adjustments for research and writing; lighter loads for first-year faculty members, and, particularly at small colleges, financial assistance for further graduate work. These practices are reported in a survey of small colleges in the south conducted by W. Starr Miller and Kenneth Wilson for the Southern Regional Education Board in 1960.[2] Except for favorable treatment shown to the first-year teacher, none of these practices directly affect teaching. Attendance at some professional meetings might well enhance teaching; attendance at others would contribute little. The standard way of getting travel money is to read a paper at a professional meeting, a practice useful enough to research but in some ways harmful to teaching. The presupposition in most of these practices is that development of greater command over a subject matter will contribute to the faculty member's general competence, of which teaching is one aspect. Even if we grant that somewhat shaky assumption, the nature of institutional support tends to slight teaching, to divert the faculty member's already fragmented attention away from the classroom, students, and learning. Few schools pay any conscious attention to the ways in which faculty members develop, sustain their efforts, or decline. My findings accord with Miller and Wilson's conclusion:

> While there are activities in these colleges directed toward establishing or improving approaches to faculty development, these activities are, in the main, uncoordinated and lacking in creativity. . . . Often reliance is placed on a limited number of relatively routine procedures and emphasis tends to be placed on procedures related to the process of orienting faculty members to the institution—an important but limited aspect of the process of development.[3]

[2] *Faculty Development Procedures in Small Colleges* (Atlanta).
[3] *Ibid.*, p. 70.

111

Various forces work against consequential faculty development programs. The most substantial force is clearly a chronic shortage of funds. The shortage at reasonably well-supported institutions is a matter of priorities. At all respectable colleges, it is a matter of not taking into account the importance of faculty development even within very slim budgets. Also, adequate salaries and fringe benefits have top priority with administrators and faculty members everywhere, and the majority of colleges and universities are chronically hard pressed to remain competitive with other professions. Despite the serious financial problems of higher education, the project still makes a strong plea for institutions to allocate a percentage of their budget specifically for faculty development.

The departmental or divisional structure of colleges and universities will undoubtedly pose resistance to any such budget allocations. Funds that disappear at the upper level of budgeting are lost to departments. In the department the greatest pressures for salaries, benefits, and minimum support of the teaching program are felt. On the other hand, departments tend to provide only the basic necessities in support of teaching, things which must be provided if an instructional program is to go on at all. But these facts of institutional operation also tend to magnify the impact of relatively small amounts of financial and other assistance from outside the department. The presence of a genuine, visible, institutional effort to assist in faculty development may have disproportionate returns in the favorable effect it has on the morale of a faculty.

Faculty development programs will probably be expected to serve many needs. We cannot expect teaching competence to develop through general provisions for faculty development. At all institutions where research is a major goal, faculty development programs should strongly emphasize teacher development. Otherwise, teaching may suffer in competition with research, for research may already be receiving the major share of outside and inside support. On many small campuses where teachers may need to improve upon subject matter competence or to keep abreast of current inquiry, a faculty development program should probably be broader in its provisions.

There have been few research attempts to conceptualize

faculty development. This lack may help explain the absence of comprehensive faculty development plans. With no clear conception of how a faculty develops, an institution may continue to do only elementary things basic to the operations of the institution. But conceptualizing faculty development is not an impossible task. Practical inquiries can be made as to the characteristics of a specific college faculty and as to the continuing research which might provide a sounder basis for action by all institutions. My studies in this respect were admittedly practical but shaped by a number of studies of faculty attitudes, job satisfactions, and career patterns. Even the use of broad chronological divisions—beginning faculty members, those in midcareer, and those close to retirement—provides a way of shaping assistance programs more likely to result in the specific improvements of teaching.

Ruth Eckert's various studies provided a solid basis for discussions of the characteristics of faculty members at these broad stages in their careers.[4] Admittedly no faculty member fits a given pattern. Yet, all go through formal preparation, take a first position, grow older, and die. Wise action within these parameters would not be a negligible achievement. Without reviewing Eckert's discussions of "young Turks," "the middle-guard," and "the old guard," this summary will single out specific suggestions for acting on what is known or can be reasonably assumed.

As regards young faculty members, career development can justifiably be seen to involve useful ways of inducting the new teacher into his first position and helpful means of fostering the development of his interest in teaching and his effectiveness as a teacher. What do new faculty members need in the way of induction? What would be most useful to their future development as teachers? The San Francisco conference stressed the following needs: (1) communicating in tangible ways the school's interest in teach-

[4] R. Eckert, "Age and the College Teacher," paper presented to Conference on Career Development, Project to Improve College Teaching, Washington, D.C., May 8 and 9, 1970; R. Eckert and J. E. Stecklein, *Job Motivations and Satisfactions of College Teachers,* Cooperative Research Monograph No. 7 (Washington, D.C.: U.S. Government Printing Office, 1961); Eckert, Williams, and Anderson.

ing; (2) explaining and clarifying the reward system; (3) informing new teachers about ways to gain knowledge and skills in teaching; (4) acquainting new teachers not only with the department but with other departments and colleagues; (5) giving the new teacher room to develop in specific ways related and unrelated to past experience; (6) using beginning teachers in a variety of ways but not using them too much; (7) making conscious efforts to offset experiences which work against development as a teacher; (8) providing specific, earmarked, reward possibilities; and (9) assisting the faltering beginner.

None of these suggestions are beyond the capabilities of most institutions. Yet, although many individual orientation practices exist, few well-defined programs are to be found. Perhaps *orientation* is not the proper word to use. Faculty members have ingrained hostilities to formal procedures taking over where informal acculturation might better serve. Nevertheless, an institution should be interested in the acculturation that does take place and in influencing it in ways favorable to the new teacher's development.

Much of the induction process is informational. Such informing goes on in various ways from the first exchange of correspondence. Candidates look at catalogs, ask colleagues about schools and departments, go about getting information on their own. During interviews, department chairmen or deans furnish additional details. Some of this information concerns teaching, though a high percentage is probably about the details of courses, load, size of classes, textbooks, testing and grading, and the like. Four aspects of the informing process need to be given particular attention.

First, candidates for positions usually receive very little information about students. As a standard practice when candidates are brought to a campus for an interview, they should be given the opportunity to appear as guest teachers in appropriate classes or in other ways to work with students as part of the interview. The purpose of this practice is not only to see candidates as teachers and to gain feedback from students on their possible appointment, but to give candidates some idea of the actual teaching environment.

Second, departments should provide an opportunity, early in the first year, for the beginning teacher and his colleagues to engage in full and open discussion of the departmental and/or college reward system.

Third, the beginning teacher needs to be informed about local resources for acquiring teaching skills. This includes not only giving directions for finding the audio-visual center but identifying individuals with certain teaching interests or skills, proffering assistance in preparing course materials, and demonstrating willingness to share classroom experiences. It should certainly include passing on information about special teaching opportunities, internal or external support of teaching, teaching awards, and possible paths of development.

Fourth, it would be wise policy to identify beginning teachers with other departments and colleagues and to get them involved in interdisciplinary work. Although a reorganization of colleges and universities will have to take place before such work can become generally possible, many ways short of reorganizing can be found to acquaint new teachers with other disciplines and departments.

We are not assuming that beginning teachers are only new Ph.D.'s fresh from graduate school. They include women and men coming into the profession from a longer experience and other careers, teachers from the public schools moving into higher education, individuals with untraditional training and backgrounds, and large numbers still working toward advanced degrees. Specific needs associated with faculty development have to be related to the kinds and circumstances of individual teachers and individual colleges.

Whatever institutional efforts are made to assist the beginning teacher, major responsibility will be placed upon the department or division and its chairman. The excellence of chairmen is in large part their ability to work with the faculty. Being able to wisely influence new members' development as teachers is a major responsibility. The chairman must acquaint himself with the new faculty member's work, not only for the help he can give but to find out how the new person's strengths fit the department's needs. The department may be able to provide different patterns of development for different talents. Most important, an informed interest in the new professors as teachers is an invitation for them to take pride in their teaching and to work at the development of their skills.

The department chairman's influence should be supported by the institution's visible efforts to make the most of its investment in the new faculty member. Funds should be made available on application for work directly connected with teaching. The necessary scholarship, thought, and imagination involved in designing a new course or trying a new method would then be tangibly encouraged.

The grants program in the state of Oregon's higher educational system is an excellent model. The present program developed out of an incentive plan for teaching in the form of money for teaching awards. Because of criticism of the teaching awards approach to instructional improvement, a substantial amount of money was made available in 1969 for instructional grants. Administrators connected with the program are convinced of its beneficial impact and presumably faculty members who received the fifty-three grants given during the first year share that belief. The University of Minnesota's Small Grants Program, initiated in 1967 by the Council on Liberal Education, is an example of a single institutional program. Proposals must be directed "to the improvement of the quality of undergraduate education" and grants have ranged from $150 to $3300. Parity with research funds is not essential to the existence of such teaching funds. There is little money available at most institutions now. A modest beginning might produce more than modest results.

Faculty development programs for young teachers should take advantage of their specific interests. At this stage, teaching is still a new and interesting subject for discussion. The development of a teaching style is for many young teachers an active concern. Getting distinguished teachers to talk about their craft, as is done in a regular series at Western Washington, is a useful way of responding to the young teachers' interests in teaching. Team teaching and other innovations are attractive to some young teachers, and a development program can facilitate and encourage such efforts. Providing the contexts within which young faculty members can engage in discussions of teaching, as simple as it seems, may be important to the development program.

116

Faculty Development

Although a faculty development program would limit its effectiveness if it concentrated solely on young faculty members, it is with young teachers that specific attention may yield the greatest returns. There also appear to be more ways in which institutions might favorably affect the individual's development early in his career. A faculty development program for beginning teachers should embrace the following:

Institutional policies should require departments to submit evidence of teaching competence or potentiality for all appointments except positions involving only research. Acceptable evidence would include recommendations from those who had observed the candidate's teaching elsewhere along with reports on observations of the candidate's performance in actual teaching situations within the department or college. Student and faculty input should be sought. "Up-or-out" practices—the hiring of large numbers of beginning teachers with the intention of keeping only a few—would be discouraged.

The institution and departments should establish programs of information for beginning teachers. These programs would give out information and enable new teachers to discuss this information with individuals inside and outside the department. Each department should hold an annual discussion, involving all members, aimed at clarifying for new members the department's and institution's written policies and established practices on retention, promotion, tenure, and salary. This discussion should be held in advance of the review of faculty personnel and should provide opportunity for revision as well as clarification of policies and practices.

Each college should establish interdisciplinary courses or committees involved in some aspects of teaching, in which new faculty members from various departments would be consequentially involved.

The department chairman or an officially designated faculty member or group should go over the new teacher's teaching assignment at the beginning of each of his first years to determine the best possibilities for furthering the individual's development as teacher while using the individual's interests and competences to best advantage in developing the department's teaching effectiveness.

117

Institutions should establish Beginning Teachers Development Grants for teachers in the first five years of their careers. Grants and awards would be publicized throughout the faculty and granted on the basis of specific proposals for improving the individual's effectiveness as a teacher or for contributing to the effectiveness of teaching in the department or university. There should be wide latitude in defining acceptable proposals, and flexibility should be maintained in the kind of support provided. Needs of different kinds of beginning teachers as well as opportunities for other kinds of faculty development should be taken into consideration.

There should be a center for teaching at each institution. Among its responsibilities would be those of assisting beginning teachers who wish to develop teaching skills and assisting departments in establishing programs for developing teaching effectiveness.

The academic vice-president or dean should establish annual programs directed at developing effective teachers. Programs might vary from year to year and include discussions of teaching practices by gifted teachers from on and off campus; opportunities for new teachers to demonstrate or discuss specific teaching practices; reviews of departmental courses and teaching by outside teams; frank discussion sessions with students about the particulars of teaching and teachers; development of specific innovative practices, such as new courses or interdepartmental alliances; the use of students and teachers in different learning contexts in which the new faculty members would be significantly involved.

Institutions should identify highly effective teachers willing to give advice about teaching to other faculty members. Formal arrangements should be minimal but the presence of these counselors should be made known to the faculty, in particular, to beginning faculty members who may wish to seek advice outside the departmental and administrative structures.

Some of these practices are being followed and many of the objectives at which they aim are being pursued in the ordinary functioning of institutions and administrators. Still, systematic faculty development efforts are needed. Formal programs are not nec-

118

essarily preferable to informal practices nor will they necessarily prove more effective. Yet the existence of a program may enable both administrators and faculty to do things which otherwise might not get done. The individual who hesitates to institute a new teaching practice may step forward within a program's framework. The cooperation often necessary to teaching innovations may be more readily forthcoming in light of a program proposal. Most of all, an institution needs visible ways of saying forcefully to its new professors, "Yes, we want good teachers, we respect good teaching, and we have specific ways of supporting them."

Midcareer faculty members are most influential in institutional policies and practices. At present, the size of this group enhances its importance. Within the universities, this group is most clearly inclined toward professional emphasis upon research and scholarship somewhat to the neglect of undergraduate teaching. At the same time, within this group are individuals who have broken free from those professional pressures who can give their energies and imagination to teaching. The problem of improving teaching among midcareer teachers in large part involves getting a reasonable share of their talents, energies, and commitment into undergraduate work. Midcareer professors constitute the largest resource with high teaching potential in higher education.

It is not easy to make specific proposals for fostering midcareer development. The sabbatical leave is important for members of this group but for faculty members in midcareer, sabbatical leaves are generally used for specific research projects rather than for increasing general teaching competence. Leaves of other kinds, again tied to scholarly accomplishments, are also available on a competitive basis to a smaller group of midcareer teachers. What might be done beyond these efforts to attract midcareer faculty members to undergraduate teaching and to maintain the commitment and effectiveness of those already functioning well as teachers?

First, various practices might be instituted which would recognize the tendency for individuals in midcareer to examine what they have been doing and to consider change. Some examples of current practices are the wide adoption of a 4-1-4 calendar plan which permits new teaching contexts; the practice at the University of California at Berkeley of placing faculty members from one department for a limited period of time in another department; and the appointment of "university" professors whose primary identification is not with any one department's specialized interests but who are committed to a larger role as teacher and educator in the university. These kinds of changes are intended to benefit not only the faculty but the students and the institution as well.

A second way to meet individual desires for a change of scene is to foster exchange programs of various kinds. Exchanges of teaching assignments with public school teachers can have remarkable impact on both parties to the exchange. The distance between small four-year and community colleges and the universities can be as great as the distance between high school and the universities. Faculty members in such institutions can also benefit from wise and active exchange. The variety of this country in its climate and geography alone affords ample opportunities. The urban storefront college, the Negro college in the South, and the back country college provide places where exchange is both possible and beneficial. It is neither excessive nor impractical to propose that a center for faculty exchange be established on a national basis to act as a clearing house for such a useful means of faculty renewal.

A final suggestion is to provide more opportunities for the kind of leadership capabilities midcareer faculty members possess and may wish to display. One obvious way is to create more collegial subunits as active centers of teaching and learning in which a variety of faculty members can achieve a closer approximation of the kind of scholar/teacher/educator they want to be. The formal cluster college has a fair chance, I think, of being widely adopted to meet the need for smaller academic communities than are to be found in large universities and colleges. This is also a way to serve students and faculty who profit by identification with a special program, whether it be honors, black studies, environmental studies, or any of a number of possibilities. Large institutions do not really need bricks and mortar, departments, degree programs and the like to create collegial units. In fact, buildings and formal programs work against the informal and transitory nature of such units, qualities that need to be preserved. What is needed are numbers of faculty members from various disciplines willing to work together to offer sufficient courses, outside activities, and objectives to give the collegial unit an identity. Midcareer faculty members are crucial to such arrangements. They are less subject to the pressures of the conventional reward system which may penalize a younger teacher's departure from ordinary departmental affiliations and scholarship. At the same time, chances for a limited number of faculty to work within a collegial structure which might, to some degree, reflect a larger philosophy of education would be particularly attractive to midcareer faculty. Many faculty members today share the student's sense of being cut off from satisfying ends. Any teaching system which processes large numbers of students limits the faculty member's knowledge of how he may be affecting any one student and of what happens to large numbers of students. Working out effective functioning subcolleges, collegial units as I have called them, is certainly not as easy as this brief sketch may suggest. But this is an innovation worth exploring and one not likely to get off the ground without leadership and participation from faculty members in midcareer.

If one considers career development in the later years, one cannot avoid "the problem of the professor of markedly diminishing effectiveness." More blunt academic usage terms this "the deadwood problem." Neither term indicates the complexity of the problem nor suggests the many kinds of individuals involved. The existence of deadwood (and the problem probably does exist on most campuses) reflects not only on those who may have become deadwood but also on those who identify the problem in that way. While one is identifying infirmities in one part of the academic body, he may be revealing callousness in another. The two problems are probably more closely related than it might seem.

Although the subject is discussed here in connection with the later years, members of any faculty age group at any time vary widely in effectiveness. To dispel the notion that deadwood is only to be found among the senior faculty we must face the stereotype bluntly. Whether we use harsh or euphemistic terminology, we are confronting a noticeable decline from a previous level of performance. Such a decline may happen at any time in a career; it need not be permanent; it may respond to diagnosis, treatment, and prevention.

There are, however, no easy solutions to the complex, affecting, and unavoidable problems which may arise as a consequence of aging. Robert Helbling, chairman of the foreign languages department at the University of Utah and author of a paper on deadwood for the Washington conference, called for an emphasis upon a developmental rather than a judgmental system for faculty personnel. Preventing faculty deterioration is preferable to trying to cure it. "A 'programme of action' in this area can obviously not be divorced from reflections on the psychology of the teacher, the process of aging, the rapidly changing student and administrative moods, the effect of the tenure and seniority systems on classroom effectiveness, the teacher's personal commitment to his calling, and the interaction of the needs for self-fulfillment and security in the teacher's career."[5]

As to specific remedies once evidences of declining performance begin to manifest themselves, these suggestions can be offered to administrators who must confront the problem:

Do not let vexations that arise from singular, troublesome cases magnify the general problem. Provide for active discourse with the faculty member reaching his later years. Try not only to relieve anxieties or to alleviate loneliness but to extend opportunities for using the last years productively and satisfyingly. Extend the period during which full or partial retirement would be customary, respected, and possible. Find ways of altering course and curriculum structures so that some older teachers can be employed to the best of their capacities as men and women of wisdom. Face up to the responsibilities that a tenure system imposes by confronting the problems which may provoke the charge that tenure protects incompetence. Factual evidence may refute such charges. Sound institutional practices can minimize the problems which do exist. Seek ways in which relationships between older faculty members and students may continue to be satisfying.

[5] "Deadwood in the Academic Forest" (Washington, D.C., May 8 and 9, 1970), p. 2.

None of the preceding suggestions can be carried out without administrative leadership. As the SREB faculty development study states, "Almost by definition faculty development procedures exist because administrators have reason for instituting them."[6]

My observations of individual colleges and universities lead me to conclude that the academic vice-president in large institutions, or the dean of the college in smaller ones, is most likely to lead in establishing campuswide faculty development programs. Such programs could, of course, be presidential programs. But presidents, though by no means as powerless as many claim to be, probably exercise their powers least in respect to academic matters. This need not be so; it should not be so. Nevertheless, there is something to be said for delegation of responsibility if an academic vice-president takes a strong and effective interest in overall faculty development. Some deans have objected to my tentative observation that leadership does not seem to be forthcoming from the deans' offices. Within large universities, the various deans seem to be more concerned with managerial duties, with acting as mediators in the allocation of funds, with building the national image of a college and protecting its local interests than with faculty development or the instructional program. However inaccurate such observations might be as applied to a particular college or university, all deans' offices could probably do more for faculty development than they are currently doing. Within an institutional faculty development program, the dean's office could be responsible for shaping and staffing the development program for beginning faculty members in the college; for establishing an informal but active counseling center for faculty members; for gathering and disseminating information about teaching; for establishing and maintaining various programs to give visibility to teaching and to enhance possibilities for the career teacher; and for setting up a review and reward system for departments based on the department's effectiveness in developing and maintaining teaching excellence.

Department chairmen have the main responsibility for the effective functioning of individual faculty members. Teaching also has the maximum chance of being recognized and rewarded within

[6] Miller and Wilson, p. 72.

department structures. There is no need to spell out the many ways department chairmen are called upon to carry out their responsibilities. But at least one additional task falls upon chairmen which is most often overlooked: that of subverting the department itself. No one is in a better position to break down the barriers that separate disciplines though it will take much more than chairmen to move American universities very far toward interdisciplinary work. Nevertheless, chairmen are in an advantageous position for exercising leadership. A man may be listened to if he appears to be arguing against his own self-interest. My visits of the past two years have not made me join those who locate most of the ills of the university in the departmental structure. Yet, I respect that position, for one cannot work very long in the university without becoming aware of the baneful influence of the department.

Departments have a very strong responsibility for the narrowness and professionalism of undergraduate programs and for the unchallenged position of specialized research in the graduate school. I have already mentioned the necessity for broadening the base for judging faculty performance beyond that which the department and department faculty provide. Implicit in what has been said about the usefulness of teaching in other departments and of interdepartmental programs is the necessity for breaking down department barriers to such efforts. Nevertheless, departments, if they have not become too large, are one of the few effectively operating sub-units that remain within the large university. Structurally, some departments suffer from being too large. Others are too small. But any reexamination of the departmental structure should find firm ways of arriving at functional groupings of students and teachers before giving up on the departments.

The department is the most efficient unit for influencing teaching practices short of working with individual faculty members. Department chairmen are in a position to work directly and effectively with the faculty. They are in a position to perceive some relationship between student development and faculty activities. And chairmen are necessarily drawn into universitywide discussions of practices and policies much more than are departmental faculty members. As I have accused presidents of failing to exercise their powers in the cause of education, I may accuse chairmen of exercising their powers to preserve departmental self-interest. If, as Clark Kerr has recently suggested, the emerging image of the president is that of academic statesman, perhaps department chairmen can emerge as statesmen, too.

Leadership is a chronic problem in all large institutions and within the collection of disparate institutions we call higher education. With respect to leadership, a quiet academic year may not be a very good sign. Certain parts of the student body seem disaffected with the very idea of leadership. Things just happen, they seem to feel; the "now" will take care of us, brothers and sisters all. Leaders become less conspicuous in quiet times. The absence of vigorous student leaders making angry demands diminishes the need for administrative or faculty leadership in response. The student riots at Columbia, for example, called forth leadership from faculty members who had never exercised that kind of leadership before. Except in times of crises, however, academic values put great emphasis upon a faculty member's being a "leader" in his field but little emphasis upon his being an educational leader within an actual academic community.

We need such leaders among the student body as well as the faculty. It would be a grave loss to higher education if the ferment aroused by student unrest of the last seven or eight years were to change to a situation where everyone chose to mind his own business. The size of the huge universities inhibits almost everyone within them from coming forward as leaders. In the small colleges a feeling of being far removed from centers of power inhibits leadership.

One way to create conditions in which leadership might arise among faculty and students is to create alternate learning structures. For many years, the honors college or program has provided an alternative attractive to faculty and students. The growth of institutes and other loosely-organized substructures is another means by which faculty members have found environments more congenial to their development. Cluster colleges constitute a third movement toward alternative structures for teaching and learning. Jerry G. Gaff's book *The Cluster College* makes this argument for the impact of such a collegiate structure:

The problem of giving adequate recognition to the teaching skills of the faculty can be resolved by creating colleges specially designed to provide an undergraduate education, attracting faculty members who are committed to this mission, creating a setting in which the effectiveness of teachers can be known by their colleagues, and giving provosts of the college a hand in deciding whether and how to reward professors.[7]

There are enough reasons in the mere growth of the universities for breaking up collegial and university structures into more meaningful subunits. There are good reasons, also, in the diversity of students and the pressures they put on the universities to provide teaching-learning communities with which students can identify. The diversity of faculty and the need to provide congenial teaching environments for them are also reasons for being receptive to alternative structures for learning. Most of all, the deliberate fostering of new structures of learning would require faculty and students to take an active part in shaping teaching and learning and would thereby increase the opportunities and possibilities for educational leadership.

Career development needs of a diverse faculty demand administrative leadership and institutional flexibility. Flexibility within an institution's reward system would not only provide more incentives to the teacher but more adequate support for other aspects of professional development. One chief fault with the reward system is that it seems to limit the ways in which one can gain prestige and material rewards. When the system is modified to include other aspects of a professor's work, it seems to propose that every professor embrace all virtues. Asked to perform as a great scholar, brilliant teacher, academic statesman, counselor to youth, and contributor to the public good, the average professor may respond by being average in all respects. Human talents and human inclinations do not exist uniformly within an individual or a profession. The reward system ought to demand less in the way of total competence and more in the way of developing that which the person can do best and wants to do best. With such a reward system, a larger number

[7] San Francisco: Jossey-Bass, 1970, pp. 234–235.

of professors might give first priority to teaching for longer periods of time.

By increasing the flexibility of practices and structures, a college might be able to make the most of the diverse talents and inclinations of faculty members and maximize the individual development of each. Respecting different kinds of teaching, providing opportunities for variety, enabling teachers to move in and out of various teaching assignments, widening the opportunities for experience in other institutions or in other careers, opening up alternatives when teachers grow stale or find certain directions blocked— these are examples of flexibility beneficial to teachers.

If one pays attention to how faculty members actually develop, how their interests change, and what specific problems present themselves, one sees the virtue of the practices suggested above. To enable teachers to move in and out of various teaching assignments, to assist them in profitable exchanges with other institutions or different kinds of institutions, to open up alternatives when teaching goes stale, and to attract different kinds of faculty members in the first place, an institution must remain flexible in many of its operating policies and practices. I do not think encouragement of such flexibility endangers stability. The whole formal structure of higher education, its traditions, and its physical facilities are on the side of stability. The formalization of such practices as have been mentioned might result in practices with greater impact upon the total faculty and even reduce the damage to the instructional program which loose but not necessarily flexible practices now create.

Another aspect of career development is the need for an assault on the myths and stereotypes which adversely affect teachers and teaching. Attention to the impressive body of research related to the evaluation of teaching may have laid some of these myths to rest. There is little factual evidence, for example, to support the notion that a teacher's popularity rests on high grades and entertainment for the students. There is no factual support for the widespread feeling that sound scholarship is incompatible with reaching large numbers of students. There is no factual evidence that competence in research has a positive or negative correlation with competence in teaching. And there is an impressive body of evidence to support the belief that some teaching practices are better than others. Careful attention to evaluation may be helping to dispel the general myth that the particulars of teaching effectiveness cannot be identified or sufficiently identified to make the development of effective teachers possible.

Unfortunately, many loose beliefs and stereotypes about teachers cluster together. Some are even supported by partial evidence. The strong belief that subject matter preparation is the only necessary preparation for a college teacher rests on the notion, acceptable to everyone, that knowing something is a requisite for teaching. It does not follow, or it should not in the minds of rational beings, that knowing more means better teaching. Most experienced teachers can testify to the usefulness of getting rid of accumulations of knowledge, can support the claim that they are teaching better because they are teaching less. But from a basic belief in the primacy of knowledge comes a host of pernicious notions: that teaching cannot be taught, that education departments are inferior educational enterprises, that involvement with pedagogy is debilitating to the mind, that teaching is an inferior calling, and that the image of teacher is not good enough in itself. Teaching practices and conditions are similarly encumbered with folklore. The faculty assumption that small classes are better for learning than large classes is opposed by the administrative conviction that size does not really matter. A large body of imperfect evidence gives comfort to both sides. On one hand, if performance on objective tests is the determinant, the size of the class does not seem to matter greatly. On the other, if one conceives of higher learning as more than learning to perform on objective tests, the question remains unanswered. The difficulty in resolving these kinds of question is that hard, factual evidence is difficult to arrive at in dealing with a problem as complex as learning in contexts that make isolating particular effects virtually impossible. Beliefs are influenced by personal needs and institutional necessities. Hard data will have to be hard indeed to show that small classes result in superior learning against the simple fact that one teacher with two hundred students serves institutional needs at a cheaper price than one with twenty.

Faculty Development

Career development operates amidst similar assumptions. Since the young seem to be the ones agitating for change, young professors must be the innovative ones. Hence the new teacher is expected to be innovative and may confuse everyone by resorting to the most traditional practices. Forgetting that innovation is in large part the result of exposure to alternatives which experience provides, we expect innovations to come from inexperienced teachers and are disappointed when they do not. At the other extreme, assuming that deadwood is coexistent with advanced years, the institution as a whole may fail to use senior faculty enough, to pose for them both the challenges and opportunities that we too often give only to the young.

Teaching needs to be given the same kind of detailed, searching, devoted attention that has been given to scholarship. Teaching cannot be passed over, in whole or in part, to specialists in education, in learning theory or in systems design. Teaching is, and must remain, the teacher's business. Only then can examination of the particulars yield results that are not locked away in the research files but which demonstrate their validity in day by day practice.

The Career Development booklet provides a more detailed discussion of matters touched upon here. It concludes with the following list of some of the constituent elements necessary to a faculty development program which aims at improving teachers and teaching:

Financial support. A specific percentage of an institution's general operating fund should go to faculty development, and specific allotment within that apportionment should go for development of teachers and teaching.

Presence of a definite system. A system does not need to embrace all activities directed toward faculty development nor does it in itself assure effective results. But the creation of some regular, continuing program with identifiable characteristics seems essential.

Lodging of responsibility with a high administratve officer. A "president's program" might be ideal. The academic vice-presidency might do as well, with major responsibilities resting with a single administrative officer.

129

The program itself should include:

Attention to the needs of beginning teachers in the form of programs to develop teaching skills.

Grants and leaves designed to be available specifically to young teachers, those in midcareer, and older teachers. These might be on a competitive basis only within each category and might be specifically designed to best attract the attention and minister to the needs of faculty members in each group.

Departmental grants for programs which promise to improve instruction or add to the competence of faculty members as teachers.

Support of teachers not attached to departments and of noncollegiate structures for learning.

Coordination with a system of teaching evaluation and assessment of student achievements.

Purposeful study and attention to the reward system within departments and the university to see that teaching rewards square with institutional policies.

Providing of information about and assistance in taking advantage of exchange programs for teachers, new teaching assignments, innovations on campus and elsewhere, and the workings of the faculty development system.

CHAPTER 8

Rewards
of Teaching

F ew spokesmen for teaching have put the case as strongly as William Arrowsmith in his keynote address to the American Council on Education in 1966. "Teaching," he said, "is not honored among us either because its function is grossly misconceived or its cultural value not understood." His advocacy is of "Socratic *teachers*, visible embodiments of the realized humanity of our aspirations, intelligence, skill, scholarship." His scorn falls most heavily upon "the pinched professionalism of the graduate schools."[1]

I will not repeat Arrowsmith's detailed analysis of causes and remedies, but variants of his arguments have been raised in every group discussion the project has held. Many faculty members seems to feel that teaching is not valued as it should be, either in the abstract or in the specific workings of the reward system. Research and publication are most often singled out as the enemy. But it is a strange sort of enemy since the majority of faculty members

[1] "The Future of Teaching," in C. B. T. Lee (Ed.), *Improving College Teaching*, p. 58.

in colleges and universities support research activities, even though many fewer than a majority do any sustained publishing.

Debate about institutional and professional practices may ignore that the values of higher education rest upon more basic considerations than promotion policies within departments. Arrowsmith charges the neglect of teaching to the "positivism of our technocratic society and the arrogance of scholarship."[2] But the causes are also antecedent to modern society and modern scholarship rooted in beliefs and pursuits which support the very development of higher education. Francis Bacon emphasized a number of strains still found in current academic beliefs. In turning upon the schoolmen, Bacon was as distrustful of trivial scholarship as is Arrowsmith. But in his advocacy of scientific inquiry and the advancement and uses of knowledge, he engages in visions that are embodied in the great university research centers which set the style for higher education today.

There is little in the advancement of science since Bacon's time that opposes the value of knowledge. To be sure, the basic argument between innocence and experience is never resolved. Yet, not until 1945 was civilization confronted with the actuality hinted at in the myths about the consequences of too much knowledge. Today, students seem far more suspicious of knowledge than are faculty members. American colleges and universities have experienced their greatest flowering as research institutions since World War II. Only an occasional voice challenges the basic belief: "Both 'knowledge' (in the sense the university intends)," John Seeley writes, "and its indiscriminate dissemination appear to be anything but useless; they are harmful, if not positively evil. . . . Western civilization lies all but dead under its own learned knife."[3] For most institutions and faculty, however, no such considerations temper the value placed upon the advancement and dissemination of knowledge as the goal of higher education.

Ann Heiss, in *Challenges to Graduate Schools,* asked 1374 members of graduate faculties in twelve disciplines in ten institutions

[2] *Ibid.,* p. 58.
[3] "The University as Slaughterhouse," in *The Great Ideas Today 1969* (Chicago: Encyclopaedia Britannica, 1969), p. 71.

to choose between three views of the nature of the university. Fourteen per cent held that the university should be detached from society and interested primarily in the value of knowledge. Position two: "the goals of a university ought to be twofold: to seek knowledge, basic to the concerns of mankind; and to provide education in intellectual analysis for those who will bring about social improvement," was chosen by 81 per cent. Less than 5 per cent took the third view that granted knowledge an intrinsic value but conceived of the university as primarily involved in defining and serving social needs.[4]

Heiss got consistent responses from various kinds of graduate institutions, more consistency, in fact, than from department to department. Faculty members in traditionally academic disciplines—English, French, history—were more inclined to view knowledge as its own reward while faculty members in economics and sociology emphasized the university's social role. It is not surprising that most faculty members took a position that embraced both the advancement and dissemination of knowledge. At the graduate level it is possible to believe in tight relationships between both research and publication and between research and teaching. But within the great majority of institutions there are conflicts in these relationships which underlie the general complaint that the reward system is hostile to teaching.

In the first place, there is a conflict between the single minded generation of knowledge and the education of a citizenry. Neither view can dominate for long. Although knowledge may be conceived of as a single pure end worth pursuing for its own sake, it is always multiple and various. There is much to know and many different ways of knowing, many consequences, foreseen and unforeseen, of knowing. In addition, knowledge as an aim of education cannot easily be considered apart from the people engaged in learning. Thus, the multiplicity and variety of knowledge is compounded by the number and variety of people involved in its pursuit.

There is no single aim for education. It is even difficult to conceive of higher educational institutions serving single purposes.

[4] Heiss, pp. 34–42.

The master plan of the state of California attempts to fulfill pluralistic aims through defining the functions of separate institutions. Community and state colleges are disseminators of knowledge; universities are the generators of knowledge. Community and state colleges deal heavily in the application of knowledge; universities deal with pure research. Community and state colleges concern themselves with advanced education for the citzenry; the university is concerned with specialized training for a professional elite. Such functional breakdowns look better on paper than they do in practice. American higher educational institutions, except at the extremes, seem determined to serve more than one aim.

Faculty members at various institutions face conflicts which complicate their choice of aims. It is impossible in many institutions to easily reconcile teaching and research, to devote oneself to the training of local citizens and to win a place in a disciplinary association devoted to the advancement of knowledge. Most colleges and universities are multipurpose institutions, many having developed from single purpose institutions such as teachers colleges, to more comprehensive designs. The act that established land grant colleges looked away from separate agricultural and mechanics colleges to schools which would offer "not only instruction for those who may hold the plow or follow a trade, but such instruction as any person might need—without the exclusion of those who might prefer to adhere to the classics." The same land grant colleges have moved steadily to higher and more comprehensive positions.

The improvement of teaching in a college desiring to improve its general position by becoming more of a generator of knowledge probably involves a greater faculty commitment to teaching and to research as well. Only in that way can faculty members of high competence be attracted to the institution and induced to stay. An individual faculty member may resent emphasis upon visible, worldly accomplishments. At the same time, he may be dissatisfied unless the institution assumes a higher place in the kingdom of knowledge.

Teaching has internal conflicts as well as conflicts with research. The kind of teaching wanted by an institution rising in the advancement of knowledge is not the same kind that suffices when training students was the sole function. In such institutions, teachers are expected to be both advancers and disseminators of knowledge. These expectations give point to Arrowsmith's contention that teaching is dishonored when the teacher has the relation to the scholar that the pianist has to the composer. Yet, Arrowsmith too easily disparages the teacher who is "merely a diffuser of knowledge or a high popularizer." In disparaging the common functions of teaching, he is limiting the possibility of teachers' achieving recognition by any means other than by moving with institutions toward the advancement of knowledge. Teaching needs to be valued on its own terms as well as in relation to individual research or an institution's research aspirations.

Research also involves faculty members in value conflicts. Faculty members do not seem unaware of the quantity of published work which comes out of a felt necessity to play the academic game rather than from any strong conviction about pursuing truth. It is hard for faculty members to sort out their motives for research. There is little possibility of a single, unmixed motive. A person who lives by his mind and prospers by what he knows may place a contribution to knowledge very high in his values. Scholarship is not all a scrambling after academic rewards. Publication may represent deep fulfillment as well as a means of moving up the academic ladder.

These conflicts are set forth to indicate some of the complexities of the values institutions and faculty members hold. Efforts to improve college teaching are strongly dependent upon the reward system within the profession and the way it operates in individual institutions. The specific values reflected in the reward system grow out of basic beliefs about the advancement and dissemination of knowledge. Stated without qualification and without regard for how they might appear in different kinds of institutions, these values appear to place teaching below research, to prize specialized competence over general learning, to measure the worth of teaching by the general level at which it is practiced, and to base a teacher's worth on the formal credentials he possesses.

These values point to the emphasis upon research and the dominance of the graduate schools. It is here that efforts at reform are most needed and are most likely to have an impact on the entire profession. Current conditions generally unfavorable to the well-being of higher education may work in favor of such reform. Student unrest has, in general, forced institutions to give more attention to the undergraduate program as has the increasing pressure for open admissions. The values of the graduate school have always been tempered by the need to educate large numbers of students. The growth of the community colleges and the shortage of positions for people with advanced degrees are two other forces working toward change. Higher education is being made aware of market limitations for persons with specialized advanced knowledge at the same time as the realization grows that higher education for all citizens is costly. Disseminating knowledge takes on increased value when it promises more jobs than does advancing knowledge. The training of citizens takes on more value when it can provide employment otherwise unavailable. But it is not sufficient to assume that necessary reforms will arise out of changing conditions. We need to closely examine some assumptions about the value of graduate work and research, about the loose application of research to every kind of inquiry, and the tendency to base judgments of worth on the accumulation of graduate credits and formal credentials.

The first step is to recognize that some university research by faculty members and graduate students is trivial and not supportable as the highest kind of activity for the numbers of highly trained men and women engaged in it. University scholars in one discipline exercise little judgment as to the value of research in another. Research proliferates through the inevitable logrolling by which research projects are permitted in one sector in order to preserve projects somewhere else. Only an affluent society tolerant of waste in most of its endeavors could sustain such an undirected, unexamined enterprise. With economic pressures limiting outside funding and legislatures beginning to realize the cost of graduate work, universities may be forced to make judgments which preserve research of great value by cutting back on research of lesser worth. These are judgments few universities are equipped to make either in terms of the values of research alone or of research as against the various other responsibilities of the university.

The central question is who is to make such judgments. If individual scholars cannot be trusted, if departments reflect the strengthened bias of individual members, if departmental colleagues outside the department fear to judge either out of a lack of competence or out of fear of damaging their own self-interests, if the university itself, in order to preserve the whole, hesitates to pass judgment on any one part, how can any judgments be made about the comparative worth of extensive research activities? And how can broader judgments be made about the comparative worth of the various obligations of the university? Considerations like these make it difficult to change the reward system as it affects the functioning of individual faculty members.

One possibility is to subject formal research and the research requirements of graduate degree work to a much more vigorous examination. A great deal of research goes on more because of the necessity of supporting graduate programs than because of the intrinsic worth of the research. Perhaps we should reverse the order in which research undertaken by graduate students is examined. The major examination would not be of the candidate on completion of his work but of the work he, his professors, and his department propose to do. Such an examination would be made by a university board and would proceed from a broad view of the university's responsibilities rather than from a discipline's traditions and practices. Such a practice might foster in graduate students and in the faculty a firmer sense of the value of various kinds of scholarly work and provide some corrective to current, wasteful practices.

An examination of the value of graduate student research from a wider point of view than that of the department engaged in the research or of the professional discipline might lead to more responsible examination of the role of research within higher education. This does not imply a need for some state, public, or high level board of control and certification, although the thought of such a board might cause due reflection about the controls and certifications which already exist within a supposedly unrestricted system. Such an examination would need to have specific criteria for judgment and to be reasonably generous in applying them. The actual value of many research activities is hard to calculate; only in medicine and supporting disciplines are results and benefits often clearly defined and widely agreed upon. In the sciences one might even accept the basic building block or jig-saw puzzle theory that makes the most of disparate and small advances within a large body of research. Scientists are conscientious in trying to keep abreast of the flood of research, trying to make the scattered information available so that it might be put to use. Science has its elegant triflers and scientists are probably the loudest in arguing for the basic worth of the free play of curiosity in the advancement of science. Still, there are enough questions about the directions, support, and uses of scientific research to justify scrutiny of scientific research in the university by men of learning outside the scientific disciplines.

In the humanities and social and behavioral sciences, the basic question of the value of research, following the analogy of the hard sciences, needs examining. The building block theory is not very applicable to the humanities. In the social and behavioral sciences, a vast amount of piecemeal research fails to make useful connections with related research or with practical applications. Moreover, results are so questionable that the amassing of data does not result in a solid foundation but often gives an excuse for starting at ground level on another new wing. In the humanities, there are quite simply many things more rewarding to do than pursuing research along scientific lines. In literature and languages, the largest field in the humanities, the trend away from philological and historical studies and the turn to criticism failed to significantly affect the research model. The pursuit of knowledge in the writing of critical dissertations (and the books of professors upon which they so heavily depend) follows the same research mode. Authoritative opinion is substituted for historical fact, the outpouring of exegetical articles substitutes for historical texts, a command of current critical jargon for a command of Old Norse or Anglo-Saxon, but in important particulars—the value of the materials being studied and the appropriateness of method to the graduate student's development as a humanistic scholar—little has changed.

University research in the graduate school cannot defend itself on the grounds that though the research may be of small intrinsic value, the training received is invaluable. This argument is similar to the older one that training in mathematics sharpens general thinking powers. For some graduate students, research is valuable training. The number for whom this is true might come close to that number who accept traditional Ph.D. requirements without complaining. This is a small number but worth encouraging if the individuals seem to develop as scholars and human beings from research training. For the larger group, a good many activities would provide a more useful means of development. In language and literature, breadth of reading is more important than depth. Depth would be more important if it were tied to a rich literature rather than to an insistence on research which immerses the student in whatever has not yet been plumbed. Synthesis, at the present point in the indiscriminate storing of knowledge, is probably an exercise superior in many disciplines to analysis. Finally, a host of important jobs need doing in the graduate student's specific preparation for teaching.

A second source of dissatisfaction with formal research is the fact that it equates all scholarship with research and implies that there cannot be learning without research—surely an untenable belief. *Research,* in its loosest meaning, is a vague term of approval which inclines people to look things up rather than think about them. The point of research of the highest kind is the emergence of some new thing or some new understanding; out of painstaking investigation the world gains something it has not had before. But a great many scholarly activities in the university are not research. To call them that or even to consider them activities in lieu of research is detrimental to a university's sense of values and to the practices of faculty members. Thinking, though it may be stimulated by research and even employed in research, is not research. Composing a symphony or writing a novel is not research, however these activities may draw upon research. Producing a play is not research nor is arbitrating a labor dispute. Reading *King Lear* for the first or the tenth time is not research nor is reading Plato or Machiavelli or Einstein or the *Journal of Abnormal Psychology.* Ministering to the mentally or physically or economically ill is not research. The range of what does not constitute research in any meaningful sense of the term is almost as wide as the universities' activities. And although the ability to engage in these many activities may have some vague resemblance to research, these activities depend more upon bringing together curiosity, passion, imagination, and intellect in ways different from the ways of research. Learning, searching (not researching)', imagining, creating, thinking, feeling, and building, to tick off a few things which may be related to research but which are not research, deserve to be valued for their own sakes.

Research should not be the single standard to which all activities outside the classroom relate. *Search* might be offered as a word which embraces more of the kinds of discoveries to be expected of higher learning. In graduate schools in many disciplines, the formal necessities of training and certifying students in research sets vast energies to work repeatedly turning over what has been turned over before. A great deal of this activity might be reduced if research became, in fact, only one of a number of activities which characterized advanced study. The graduate school which gave up the fiction that every student must make a genuine contribution to knowledge and substituted such possibilities as synthesizing existing knowledge or creating in any of the arts or transmitting research into professing, or even just exposing, in some effective way, the fruits of one's years of study would do both research and scholarship a great service. Research and scholarship are not synonymous. The limited demands of research have probably ruined as many potentially great scholars as they have made wise.

These arguments resist the established notion that the higher one goes up the formal educational ladder, the better; and that such an advance necessitates specialization and certification. The former notion is almost impossible to argue against; its workings show themselves clearly in our whole system of education. In salary, public respect, and professional prestige, the scale clearly goes up from elementary school teacher to full professor in a major university. Such a scale recognizes, to a degree, individual excellence. But it just as surely imposes limitations on the recognition accorded excellence. Official degree credentials not only identify but fix the individual in his place on that scale. They become more than indications of educational achievement. They shape the nature of that achievement. They support the division between undergraduate and graduate education, a division which may stand in the way of healthier relationships between disciplinary research and broad educational experience.

Conflicts between graduate work and undergraduate education, the advancement and dissemination of knowledge, research and teaching are all aspects of the values which underlie long established practices in higher education. As a result of these conflicts, the reward system will continue to engender complaints about adverse effects on teaching. Faculty and students will continue to carry out teaching and learning functions amidst a general discontent over university priorities.

How can the reward system be changed? The project's career development booklet makes this summary observation:

> It seems reasonable to say that if the reward system is to change in ways more favorable to teaching, criteria for advancement must be more precisely defined, judgments on performance more broadly based, and an avowed intention to reward teaching carried out in practice. Procedures for advancement will probably become more formal, and policies will have to be set forth more openly and in greater detail.[5]

What the institution expects of its faculty and programs needs to be clarified at all levels. Fred Luthans' study of promotion policies at forty-six large state universities found that almost all had central promotion policies. However, only half of the central administrators reported policies which were spelled out and known by everyone, and only a third of the faculty members so regarded them.[6] There may be no escaping vagueness in stating central university goals. But precisely stated criteria for advancement consistent with central aims can be set forth in writing at the department level. Actions at the various levels of review can be made in light of central goals and departmental criteria.

The adoption of evaluation instruments and procedures and

[5] Eble, *Career Development,* p. 85.
[6] *The Faculty Promotion Process* (Iowa City: University of Iowa Bureau of Business and Economic Research, 1967), pp. 44–47, 60–63.

the actions of deans and department chairmen are crucial to making a reward system work as it was intended to. Faculty members involved both in judging and in being judged face an internal conflict between attachment to the informal and imprecise procedures they deem to be appropriate to academic life and the need for objective and precise measures. Responsibility falls on administrators to see that policies square with practices. In view of chronic discontent, however, explicit and efficiently functioning systems may not be enough. Judgments other than those of the departments may need to be brought into the system. Central goals may be better stated through financial priorities than official rhetoric.

Departments and departmental faculty members have an indispensable role in evaluating colleagues. Sources of data and judgment should also come from outside the department, and institutional policies should ensure that such information is effectively used. Student input as to teaching ability is an example of such data. Teaching outside the department provides another source. Deans and review committees provide a mild check on departmental actions. These measures are not very strong in the face of the department's powers. The creation of teaching structures and positions outside the departmental structure, budget, and values is a counter force that could have consequential effects in rewarding teaching.

The administration resolute enough to create a number of nondepartmental learning structures and teaching positions might also be willing to share budgeting responsibilities with the faculty. Exact and open accounting may be the only way institutions can be brought to recognize where their priorities are rather than where they are professed to be. Only at the top of the budget is it possible to allot substantial funds for faculty development.

Funds from the general budget could well go to support individual grants for purposes directly affecting teaching and for a center for teaching and learning which could serve diverse needs. Grants should foster small improvements as well as large and should be earmarked in specific ways to prevent their being competitive across the faculty. Grants are probably a better expenditure of funds than teaching awards. Although such awards are useful, they provide neither substantial support for teaching nor evidence of an administration's willingness to give that support. A center for teaching is necessary to gather and disseminate information about teaching and to provide incentives, encouragement, and support of teaching. It should not be a research center, and it should particularly involve members of the faculty outside those professionally concerned with education.

One last word about the general value attached to teaching. How does one combat the idea that really first-rate teaching and the work that goes into preparing new courses or innovative teaching do not take any more time than merely competent teaching? If we prize first-rate teaching, it makes no more sense to reduce the teaching load in favor of research than to reduce it in favor of teaching. There is no exact measure of how much teaching constitutes an adequate teaching load. But when a teacher is trying to restructure his course or his teaching or is trying to teach even one class in ways that constantly place demands on his learning, his powers of thought and imagination, and his time and energy, teaching consumes great quantities of time. Time, moreover, is demanded during the school term; it can be taken care of only in part during the professor's free time in the summer. This is the kind of teaching that institutions must somehow recognize as worth encouraging and supporting. The reward system must have the internal flexibility and room—in compensation and in time—to make teaching worth a faculty member's full commitment. The accepted use of released time for research, at least within the university, assumes that something of value will emerge. As has been argued at length in this chapter, for large numbers of professors, considering their individual talents and interests and the range of worthwhile things to be done, research does not provide an adequate field of operation. Without hurting the prospects for research, the rewards and values of extraordinary teaching could become much more visible and enhance the entire higher educational enterprise.

CHAPTER 9

The Teaching Environment

᪽᪽᪽᪽᪽᪽᪽᪽᪽᪽᪽᪽᪽᪽᪽

One of the project's major objectives was to inquire into working conditions which would motivate or enable faculty members to function well as teachers—"optimum working conditions." The study was completed by Jerry Gaff and Robert Wilson, research psychologists at the Center for Research and Development in Higher Education of the University of California at Berkeley.[1] In addition to particular findings summarized here, the study achieved two important results: it directed attention to the concept of the teaching environment as a significant factor in attempts to improve teaching, and it emphasized the need to give research attention to the particulars which affect faculty performance.

The shift from "optimum working conditions for effective teaching" to "teaching environment" is more than an improvement in expression. It also signifies a broadening of the concept. Working conditions are realities teachers cannot escape, but the term tends

[1] *The Teaching Environment,* mutilith (Washington, D.C.: American Association of University Professors and Association of American Colleges, 1971).

144

to focus attention on tangible, extrinsic forces which affect performance. Teachers are not free from the large impact of these forces but their work also responds to intrinsic motivations and satisfactions that are characteristic of the service professions.

The Gaff-Wilson study has added to our understanding of what may specifically motivate faculty members as teachers. Their research incorporated data from two recent interview studies of selected faculty members at different types of collegiate institution. Three general aspects of the working environment were identified as particularly important for teaching: (1) nature of the student body, (2) character of faculty colleagues, and (3) institutional policies and practices with respect to teaching. What a faculty member does as a teacher may be closely related to the impact of these aspects of the teaching environment.

The student body in this country's colleges has always been diverse but it has probably become more diverse in the past few years. Pressures to meet the supposed needs of a more diverse student body have greatly increased. Like many things that catch headlines and some things which take up the attention of faculty members, the increased visibility of Blacks, Chicanos, Indians, and the poor within higher education is disproportionate to the actual increase in their numbers. Nevertheless, few colleges can escape recognition of the needs of these individuals who give more scope to the term *student*. Together with pressures to break away from narrowly defined college-age groups and the pressures of a noticeable minority on every campus who self-consciously set themselves against the traditional student concept, there are potent forces making faculty members think of students as something other than younger images of themselves.

Diversity has already caused many problems for institutions and faculty members. Is Black Studies to be a separate program staffed exclusively by black staff members? Are black students' needs to result in advertent or inadvertent neglect of other minority groups? How can teaching practices, particularly grading and accrediting, be reconciled with students who have dubious respect for the value of tradition, study, and credentials? How can huge, diverse student bodies find communities for learning? How many

145

aims can a university serve? Are departures from policies and practices to meet the needs of students wise adaptations or are they
chiefly copouts and sellouts?

One good outcome of facing the insistent questions raised by
a diverse student population will be a change in undergraduate education away from the tendency to regard the best students as future
professionals and the others as destined to fill slots in an established
job order. If this shift in viewpoint comes about it will be in part
because collegiate institutions have found ways to make student
visions concrete. These visions include the general concept of community—less distance between formal and informal learning, closer
connections between the academy and the world outside, a wider
variety of work, and new work or working conditions which dignify
man.

An important part of the present generation of students is
accurately described in the Gaff-Wilson report as "better prepared,
more socially and politically aware, less passive in educational style
and expectations, and more demanding of participation in the decisions which affect the course of their education."[2] These students
seem to have created distance between students and faculty. In my
discussions with students and faculty, regardless of the calibre of the
school I was visiting, there seemed to be a constant distance between
student perceptions and faculty perceptions on many aspects of
teaching and learning.

Professors seemed to overestimate what students knew or
should know. Students seemed to underestimate what professors
were interested in. Professors were as vexed with the student's idea
of relevance as the students were with the faculty's concept. Professors resented the intimacy the students seemed to demand while
students chafed at the professors' lack of concern. Professors insisted
upon exercising their own freedoms but remained hostile to the students' exercise of theirs. It is difficult to avoid dwelling on the distances between faculty and students as a mark of our age but it
may be wiser to consider that there are always distances between
faculty and students. The teacher's task is always to draw reluctant
students to learning. The malaise some professors now feel may be

[2] *Ibid.,* p. 35.

simply a reflection of how easy they have had it as teachers in the past.

A Berkeley professor told Jerry Gaff: "I used to feel like one of the students. Now I'm not one of them anymore. I feel almost in an adversary position. Perhaps I have stopped changing. They have a different concept of the university than I have been taught to believe in. They have changed for the better. I admire them. I respect them more but teaching is more difficult. The things that used to work two years ago don't work anymore."[3] This statement is as interesting for what it implies about the past as for what it says about the present. What faculty members regarded in the past as a shared concept of the university may have been chiefly a set of faculty assumptions students were not allowed to question. The successful faculty member used to move steadily and speedily to teaching only students who fit his own professional aspirations and expertise. Anxieties that have arisen among faculty members about no longer being able to work with students is less a new condition than a return to teaching which has always had to work against a common ignorance.

Teachers like students who are like themselves. When conditions afford the opportunity, teachers gravitate to such students, away from mass remedial instruction typical of the fifties, away from freshman and sophomore survey courses, away from the unacademic, the uncommitted, the unprofessional students. The economic realities of the moment may bring some teachers back to these less desirable tasks. If teachers can face these tasks with generosity and with a sense of the larger opportunities inherent in working where the effects of deprivation and ignorance are most serious, more important higher learning can be the result.

But college faculty are not only pushed by the diversity of students and by the wider range of these students' needs, they are being pushed by a general desire for close, personal teaching. The formal distance a brilliant lecturer maintains between himself and the large number of students attracted to his classrooms may be a necessary protective device. Meeting with students, working with them, helping them develop their minds and personalities is time-

[3] *Ibid.,* p. 35.

consuming, fatiguing work. Teachers who draw their greatest job satisfactions from students tend to invest great amounts of time and energy in working with students. These teachers also tend to feel that they do not receive adequate compensation for the effort involved. There is evidence that such teachers have a disproportionate impact on students. In reviewing two decades of research into how students change within college settings, Arthur W. Chickering offers a hypothesis that "when student-faculty interaction is frequent and friendly and when it occurs in diverse situations calling for varied roles, development of intellectual competence, sense of competence, autonomy, and purpose are fostered."[4] If college teachers are to continue to find working with students a major source of satisfaction (and I do not see how learning can prosper if they do not), teachers must adapt to diversity, to changing goals, and to desires for more interaction between student and teacher.

Colleagues are an extremely important part of the teaching environment. A study of faculty members at University of California at Davis found that teachers who were interested in teaching were better teachers. The finding, stated that sparsely, is a truism. Some details of the research need to be pointed out. By various means, the researchers identified some teachers on the Davis faculty who were regarded as good teachers and some who were not. They then subjected both groups to extensive questioning about what they did as teachers: time given to preparation, making up tests, keeping current in their fields, and so on. The interviewers did not know whether individual faculty members had been identified as good or poor teachers. When the data were processed and compared with identifications of good and poor teachers, few items distinguished one from the other. One cluster which did distinguish the good teachers were items which revealed an active interest in teaching. Discussing teaching with colleagues was one manifestation of this interest.

In some ways, this finding is as discouraging as it is encouraging to the improvement of teaching. Good teachers talk to other good teachers. The common phenomenon of like attracting

[4] *Education and Identity* (San Francisco: Jossey-Bass, 1969), p. 153.

148

like increases the chance that useful cross-fertilization between good and bad teachers will not take place often enough. Colleagues are in a strong position to affect the teaching performance of other colleagues. The superior teacher does not just assume his role when he steps into the classroom. The superior teacher can talk about and exemplify many of the particulars of his teaching. Given the right contexts (and from what has just been said these contexts will not come into being by natural processes), superior teachers might exercise more influence on their colleagues than they now do.

The contexts which now exist make small use of colleague-to-colleague relationships. Team teaching is probably the most common practice which exposes one teacher to the style of another. Wherever I have heard it discussed (in the University of Iowa English department, for example), it has been praised for its impact upon the faculty. The common practice of placing beginning teachers with experienced teachers might well be supplemented by more opportunities for senior professors—from different as well as from the same disciplines—to teach together. One difficulty about these arrangements is economic. Two professors in a classroom are more expensive than one. But there are ways both of reducing and justifying the expense. Increasing the number of students has always been the way to pay for instruction. There is at least a possibility that a number of professors might handle a larger class better than a single professor. There should also be some division of labor within a team-taught class which would lessen the workload for the individual professor by comparison with a class for which he had sole responsibility. Faculty and administration should recognize these possibilities. In addition, if an institution took the responsibility for developing the potential of its faculty as teachers seriously, the extra cost of team-taught courses could legitimately be charged off to faculty development rather than to the cost of instruction.

There remain difficulties in getting faculty members to enter into teaching arrangements which may violate their personal beliefs about the privacy of the classroom and which may require more classroom management. The example of colleagues who do not draw back either from the extra work or from the exposure involved may be the best way of affecting a large portion of the faculty.

Teachers able to set examples can be found on every campus and they are probably not used as much in this respect as they could be. Informal programs can overcome the reluctance of some excellent teachers to demonstrate their expertise. Increasing the opportunities for informal discussions of teaching may be as successful as instituting formal programs. Drawing on colleagues from nearby colleges and universities may be a way of getting around the rivalries and familiarities which might detract from the effectiveness of campus colleagues.

Studies of various kinds of institutions seem to indicate that schools concerned with teaching undergraduates tend to have more collegial relationships among the faculty. The Gaff-Wilson report argues that such schools seem to have maintained "something which approximates a community of scholars. It seems reasonable that if one wants to enhance the environment for teaching he should try to create a community in which close personal relationships are cultivated among the faculty and between faculty members, administrators, and students, and in which as many people as possible are encouraged to participate in decisions affecting the life of the group."[5] The open university is more than a loose concept being forced upon the university by undisciplined youth; it is a necessity if universities are to function as teaching-learning communities.

The difficulty in arriving at such a community or at communities within a large university framework, is probably chiefly that of bringing students and faculty together in achieving goals meaningful to both. Outside the department major and the professional programs, there are few such common goals. Even the bonds of the department or professional school are not very strong for many students today. Conditions may be right, however, for entering once again into interdisciplinary work, a pious hope for decades against the steady drift toward specialization. The awareness of ecology, the pressing need for social communities, the very size of many universities, may have increased the receptivity of faculty members to programs of study which do not confine themselves within disciplines or which break away completely from a subject matter focus. The qualified success of cluster colleges, the

[5] *The Teaching Environment*, p. 49.

pressure from some students for free universities, the loosely structured experimental colleges of diverse kinds, may point the way to learning communities within the larger college or university framework. A teaching-learning community in which the dynamics of learning would be taught and practiced would be one kind of community. Pressure from common needs and common interests might create others. In any event, the ideal of community is inescapably present today, and teaching may benefit from its presence.

It should not need saying, but it does, that departments can establish strong and beneficial colleague relationships. A good department is one in which such relationships create attitudes and responses toward teaching-learning which are broader than the attitudes and responses of individual members and which go beyond the parochialism which is at its worst in bad departments. Departments fragment knowledge, create and sustain vested interests, and stand in the way of university aims which clash with departmental self-interest. They mirror the worst qualities of nationalism in the larger political world. At the same time, they break up the mass which makes group enterprise possible. One of the aims of establishing communities of teachers and students along other than departmental lines would be to stimulate departments to make the most of the communities traditional structures have created.

Direct institutional support of teaching is regrettably weak. Informal written questionnaires, interviews, and my own discussions on individual campuses support this observation. The Gaff-Wilson interviewers asked faculty members, "Does this school do anything to encourage good teaching?" Typical first responses were "Not that I'm aware of," "Very little," "What do you mean?" and "Some people talk about it, but nobody does much." Given more time to think about the question, faculty members did think of things which were being done to encourage good teaching, but most were judged ineffective. Distinguished teaching awards, for example, are found on many campuses, but opinion is about equally divided as to whether or not they foster good teaching.

To the extent teachers are employed, offices and classrooms provided, management structures efficiently operated, student credit hours produced, and degrees conferred, institutional support of

151

teaching is fundamental to university operations. But provisions for something beyond the necessaries—encouragement, incentives, rewards—these are not regular and substantial parts of college or university functioning. The department is probably assumed to be the place where teaching receives this kind of support. But departments are locked into a system and a budget which limit its concerns to seeing that classes are staffed, not necessarily that they are taught well. Neither department nor university efforts go much beyond this as is indicated by the fact that faculty members, fully engaged in teaching, respond so equivocally or negatively when asked if teaching is given support.

Their response may be blamed, in part, upon the apparent workings of the reward system. In crucial matters of appointment, retention, promotion, salary increases, and tenure, quality teaching has not received the careful consideration it deserves. As a result, faculties tend to express cynicism toward specific but less significant efforts to support or encourage good teaching. Evaluation of teaching, upon which a more favorable reward system might rest, is about as dubiously regarded as participation in committee work. It may be accepted as a necessity but it is not a responsibility faculty members face gladly. Finally, institutional policies do not unequivocally support teaching. Statements about advancement policies are far from clear and practices are far from precise in carrying out policies which may or may not be favorable to teaching.

Some of the blame rests with the obvious physical support given teaching. Teachers, like other individuals, are often unduly vexed by little things. The condition of classrooms in most colleges and universities does not create a feeling that the system is steadily and sensitively concerned with teaching. It is argued by some teachers that a ten thousand dollar machine is easier to come by than a supply of chalk and erasers. Heating units that don't work, floors which don't get swept, equipment which doesn't function, and red tape which has to be cut through in any attempt to move teaching out of its ordinary routines—all adversely affect a teacher's perception of how well teaching is supported.

Comparisons inevitably arise, many of them unfair, to support the feeling that teaching and teachers are neglected. Laboratory equipment for the sciences is costly. The total cost is directly proportional to the amount of high level research going on. Although teachers in the sciences may complain about a lack of equipment for classroom use, they often do so because they sense that some colleague somewhere may be getting an expensive piece of apparatus without having to hammer away incessantly at the dean. Secretarial services, when the faculty member wanders through the administrative halls, seem to be in evidence everywhere. Yet when he returns to his department, no private secretary awaits him. Often there is not an adequate secretarial pool to take care of the large amount of written clerical work required in teaching. Every young faculty member quickly learns the channels for getting research funds; part of his graduate training has been in finding and tapping sources outside the university. The faculty member interested in enlarging his knowledge of, grasp of, or extension of teaching has great difficulty finding such sources of support.

The apparent defects in institutional support for teaching arise partly from a lack of tangible means of support and partly from things which magnify the deficiency in the minds of teachers. Both work against the encouragement of teaching which would rise above the ordinary. Another force dispiriting to the ambitious teacher is public opinion reaching the faculty through boards of trustees and university administrations. Teachers in colleges and universities, like teachers in the public schools, simply cost too much. The stress on accountability, the attacks on tenure, and the direct interest of legislators in teaching loads, are all evidence of that basic public perception.

We are probably dealing with a fundamental condition of education in America. Aspirations are high and costs mount in relation to those aspirations. The growth of community colleges is a phenomenon that has escaped the attention of many people in the four-year colleges and universities. Many of these institutions are shoestring operations; the majority have respectable physical facilities and pay faculty well. Almost all are supported by public monies and they add to the financial demands made on the public. Of course it is possible to pay the costs of education if we would just shift our priorities. But it does not seem likely that priorities will shift, or if they do shift, that financial support for higher education will improve strikingly.

In consequence, institutional policies and practices must always stretch resources and sharply curtail what institutional policies and practices might do for teaching. Whether or not collective bargaining will become a prominent force for achieving equitable salaries and related benefits for faculty members, there is no certain connection between such negotiations and achievements and improvements in teaching. I have no intention of setting aside, in this discussion, the importance of salaries, benefits, and basic working conditions. When faculty members feel they are underpaid, overworked, or simply not given sufficient institutional support, they are likely, consciously or unconsciously, to put less time, energy, and skill into teaching. If teaching is assumed to be capable of being stretched to fit any number of students, teachers can be assumed capable of adjusting to that stretch by diminishing their efforts. In either event, the quality of teaching goes down.

Institutional support which ultimately depends on public or private funds is hampered by public misunderstanding about how much work a faculty member does as well as about the kind of work he does. The supposed response of a legislator who was told that a professor at the university had a 12-hour load—"Well, that seems to be a fair day's work"—becomes pertinent when legislatures begin to set minimum teaching load figures for state institutions. Time in the classroom is only a part of teaching responsibilities and teaching in a majority of colleges and universities is only a part of the work expected of the professor.

Getting faculty attention centered upon teaching often involves a struggle with other important professional duties. Teaching cannot stay vital without enlightened scholarship and practice. We may be critical of the value of much of the research that goes on under university auspices but we cannot very well be critical of the curiosity which motivates inquiry (not necessarily formal research) or of the connection between teaching and the inquiring mind. Moreover, as publishing scholars are quick to point out, printed materials are often a form of teaching. A good textbook reaches many more students than the teacher may personally reach in a lifetime. Nevertheless, teaching and research are not always and in every subject complementary activities. Failure to recognize how and when they will compete for a faculty member's attention is failure to recognize an essential characteristic of the college professor's work.

But a college professor's life is not simply divided between research and teaching. Advancement policies in a majority of institutions include service as a major responsibility. Service includes as wide an array of activities as does teaching. Service extends from assisting the department's functioning to the performance of important community activities related to university work. Professional recognition is sometimes regarded as a separate category. It includes awards received, positions held in professional societies, and the like. Administrative duties may also be a separate advancement category. In large departments, there may be a number of important administrative assignments which fall short of being full-time. Since faculty members move in and out of full and part-time administrative jobs, many faculty members must consider their administrative competence inseparable from their total professional worth as teachers and researchers.

The time and energy a faculty member gives to any or all of these activities is affected by the institution's supporting policies and practices. The conclusion that development efforts for the faculty as teachers are very limited is partly due to the fact that faculty development plans which do exist spread their benefits to cover all these aspects. Teaching does not rank very high either in terms of institutional support or in the choices faculty make when given an option. Institutional policies and practices vary widely but few give support to teaching outside that provided within departments to see that classes are met.

The common term *teaching load* casts some light upon the way teaching is regarded. The very commonness of teaching—that which almost everyone does as an essential condition of employment —emphasizes its position somewhere between what one has to do and what he wants to do. Teaching has also been made to fit accounting procedures which stress the obligatory nature of the activity. Teaching may well be a second choice for those who make college professing a career. Teaching enables many practitioners—scientists, painters, writers, musicians, and others—to pursue their primary, nonteaching interests until success allows some of them to escape teaching altogether. Teaching supports great quantities of advanced scholarly work in all disciplines which society would not support in more direct ways. Add to these the basic dilemma that teaching demands that the teacher somehow harmonize the full development of his intellectual and imaginative understanding with the limited understanding of the students he confronts and we begin to see why teaching may be regarded as a load and at times a burden.

The effects of the teaching environment are reflected in the satisfactions teachers derive from their work. Job satisfactions vary not only with individuals but according to the kind of institution. In general, universities and schools aspiring to be universities or competing with universities for faculty and students have faculty members who gain greatest job satisfaction from the opportunity to pursue scholarly work. Faculty members in state colleges and four-year colleges gain marked satisfaction from teaching but express strong dissatisfaction with underemphasis on research. Only in community colleges are teaching and working with students in other ways clearly the major source of satisfaction. The ideal teaching load at research-oriented universities may seem to approach zero but even there, most faculty members want to continue to do some teaching.

The attitudes of most faculty members toward teaching and research are probably more favorable than toward service and much more favorable than toward the details of governance and administration which faculty members cannot escape. Their relationship to administrative details is a love-hate one. Although faculty members have insisted on an increasing role in university governance, they apparently have not found great satisfactions in performing these duties. The faculty attitude toward the details of running the university is that no one wants to perform them but few faculty members are willing to leave them to someone else. In surveys of job satisfactions among Minnesota college faculty members, Ruth Eckert found in 1956 and again in 1968 that about a third of the faculty expressed a desire to spend less time on committee and administrative work. By contrast half the university faculty members wanted more time for research and one-fourth more time for teaching.[6]

The Eckert studies are probably our best source of information about how faculty members spend their time in different kinds of institutions and about what kinds of changes have been taking place in disposition of time and in the attitudes of faculty members toward their work. Generalizations about the faculty in higher education are less accurate than generalizations about faculty within different kinds of institutions and at specific periods of time. Although the Eckert studies were confined to colleges and universities in Minnesota, they included thirty-three different institutions (forty-three in 1968 because of an increase in junior colleges)' and at least one example of the kinds of institutions found nationally. A summary of some of her findings will conclude this discussion of the teaching environment.

University faculty members seem to be increasingly attracted to an academic career because it promises a congenial style of life. Eighty-four percent of those responding to the 1968 survey named favorable working conditions or a desire to take part in college academic and social life as major reasons for choosing an academic career. The figure in 1956 was 66 per cent. Among the more specific reasons given were the intellectual challenge of university work and the desire to pursue research. Both reasons were cited by about half the respondents. Desires to work with college-age students and to "contribute to the field by college teaching" were named by about 30 per cent. These figures shift considerably for the state-college faculty and the community-college faculty. The general direction of this shift was away from intellectual challenge and research and toward reasons associated with the philosophy or purpose of the institution (the sample includes a good number of schools with religious affiliations). In the community colleges, particularly, reasons cited frequently were directly associated with teaching. General atmosphere, most frequently cited by state college faculty as a source of job satisfaction, was noted least often by those in the community colleges.

[6] Eckert, Williams, and Anderson, p. 17.

Teaching activities at all institutions take up the largest share of a faculty member's time. At the university, the median time spent on teaching by faculty respondents was 45 per cent, but individual faculty members reported less than 20 per cent and as much as 100 per cent. The percentage of time expended on teaching went up at state colleges and community colleges. The median figure was 66 per cent for liberal arts college faculties and 71 and 80 per cent, respectively, for state and community college faculties.

Research was much more characteristic of the university faculty than of the faculty in other institutions. The median figure for time invested in research by university faculty was 20 per cent. Only 21 per cent of the university staff reported no current research activities, as compared with 45 per cent for private liberal arts college faculty, and 60 and 77 per cent, respectively, for state and community college faculties.

Faculty members at the university reported 10 per cent less time given to teaching in 1968 than in 1956. Two out of three faculty members at the university favored giving more time to research rather than to teaching or to contacts with students outside of class. This change has also been noted in Harold Hodgkinson's 1970 study of institutions in transition, state colleges of various kinds moving toward university status: "As the comprehensiveness of a school increases, commitment toward teaching decreases . . . hours spent in teaching have declined for all five types of institutions; the more comprehensive schools show a more dramatic decline, however, than do the two year colleges."[7]

Faculty members expressed a high degree of satisfaction with their choice of career. At the university level, opportunities for research and intellectual stimulation slightly outweighed opportunities to work with college-age youth and liking for teaching as sources of satisfaction. At other institutions, research and intellectual stimulation were of considerably less significance. Among other items mentioned, two seem to have most significance. Interesting colleagues and associates were frequently cited by university faculty but were cited much less often by community college faculty. Satis-

[7] *Institutions in Transition* (New York: Carnegie Commission on the Future of Higher Education, 1970), p. 83.

factions based on financial or professional recognition of faculty services rose significantly (from 22 per cent to 38 per cent) among university faculty from 1956 to 1968.

Dissatisfactions with aspects of college teaching careers focused on poor relations with colleagues, administrative red tape, and inadequate facilities. Low salaries were cited as sources of dissatisfaction by only 12 per cent in the 1968 study as contrasted with 50 per cent in the earlier one. Complaints did not differ greatly from one institution to another. The university faculty felt more strongly, however, about administrative red tape.

In general, these statistics square with other studies. Excessive teaching load and low salaries, sources of chronic complaints from faculty members, appear to be less vexing today. Teaching loads have gone down steadily through the past two decades. A six to fifteen hour range would cover the schedules of most of the faculty employed at a wide range of institutions. The AAUP, in response to numerous appeals over the years, published guidelines for faculty workloads in 1970. When the statement came before the national meeting for approval in 1969, it was referred back to the committee chiefly because of objections that the recommended teaching load figures were excessive. The revised statement, accepted in 1970, sets maximum load figures at twelve hours per week for undergraduate instruction and nine hours for instruction partly or entirely at the graduate level. Preferred teaching loads are nine and six hours respectively. The introductory paragraph of the AAUP statement is worth quoting for what it says about this basic aspect of the college teacher's working conditions:

In the American system of higher education, faculty "workloads" are usually described in hours per week of formal class meetings. As a measurement, this leaves much to be desired. It fails to consider other time-consuming institutional duties of the faculty member, and, even in terms of his teaching, it misrepresents the true situation. The teacher normally spends far less time in the classroom than in preparation, conferences, grading of papers and examinations, and supervision of remedial or advanced student work. Preparation, in particular, is of critical importance, and is probably the most unremitting of these demands: not only preparation for specific classes or conferences, but that more

159

general preparation in the discipline, by keeping up with recent developments and strengthening his grasp on older materials, without which the faculty member will soon dwindle into ineffectiveness as scholar and teacher. Moreover, traditional workload formulations are at odds with significant current developments in education emphasizing independent study, the use of new materials and media, extracurricular and off-campus educational experiences, and interdisciplinary approaches to problems in contemporary society. Policies on workload at institutions practicing such approaches suggest the need for a more sophisticated discrimination and weighting of educational activities.[8]

Salaries have also achieved levels which remove some of the strains so evident in the fifties, but the movement to collective bargaining is evidence of a continuing felt need to remain competitive within the national economy. Salary differentials, with respect to which private liberal arts colleges are at a disadvantage with state colleges and universities, tend to emphasize the importance of university value standards. Public community colleges, however, have considerable economic advantages over other segments of higher education since they have more faculty positions available and salary scales are as good as or better than salaries at the liberal arts colleges.

Reasonable workloads and adequate salaries are fundamental necessities if college teaching is to attract the kinds of personnel and to get from them the kind of commitment that develops and maintains teaching excellence. Gaff and Wilson suggest a number of other ways in which institutions can help create a favorable environment for effective teaching:[9]

First, faculty members should be aware of general developments in higher education, especially developments directly related to teaching and learning. College professors are usually well trained in their academic disciplines but most are not trained in education. They learn the theory and practice of higher education, if at all, on

[8] "Statement on Faculty Workload," in *AAUP Policy Documents and Reports* (Washington, D.C.: American Association of University Professors, 1971), p. 62.

[9] *The Teaching Environment,* pp. 56–63.

the job. Colleges and universities should take special steps to see that the teaching faculty knows about current educational criticisms, research findings, change proposals, and innovative programs.

Second, there should be a visible comprehensive program to assist the personal and professional development of faculty members. The faculty is the single most important and most costly part of the instructional program. Colleges should have a high interest in their teachers and should protect their investment by doing all they can to aid the development of effective teaching as professors move along in their careers.

Third, there should be provision for faculty members to obtain useful feedback from students concerning their teaching activities. Student feedback is important because it helps a teacher learn to develop more effective teaching skills and strategies and because it allows him to derive personal satisfaction from the achievements of students.

Fourth, there should be periodic reviews of the instructional program and proposals for its improvement. Programs, like people, tend to change with the passage of time. Even if it does not grow out-of-date, a program may fall into a comfortable routine. Periodic review can revitalize an established program while providing a basis for the development of new ones.

Fifth, there should be institutional policies and procedures favorable to the creation of alternative teaching and learning environments which transcend the limitations of such traditional concepts as a self-contained campus, a curriculum isolated from the rest of student life, a fragmented disciplinary approach to teaching, standardized courses, and a single program. Innovative contexts alongside traditional settings may allow higher education to provide a variety of environments to meet the diverse needs of students, teachers, and society.

CHAPTER 10

Is Teaching
Obsolete?

~~~~~~

Throughout the course of this project, I faced a question which struck at the very nature of what I was trying to accomplish. Sometimes the question was not a question but an assertion that in focusing on teaching, I was misdirecting my efforts. The emphasis, I was told, should be on learning. To some, learning is like heat, the only phenomenon. Teaching, like cold, has no reality except as a concept useful to laymen. Some students were also distrustful of teaching but for different reasons. Often these students had been caught up in one of the spontaneously-generating learning experiences which substitutes group process and independent growth for a teacher's instruction. My own beliefs with respect to teaching and learning are set forth in the final paragraph of *The Recognition and Evaluation of Teaching:*

> Teaching can scarcely be talked about these days without having someone object that the focus should be on learning. My own belief is that teaching-learning are two sides of a coin. The whole is what we want, but we can still fruitfully contemplate either side. The project's interest in evaluation forces us to look

at both sides, though the area examined is but a small part of the configuration of either teaching or learning. If evaluation can contribute to bringing the campus together in the common teaching-learning enterprise, if it can put some life into daily routines, if it can work specific improvements upon individuals and contribute to what we know about teaching and lead us to act on that knowledge, then it is surely worth the risks and effort it may involve.[1]

What this paragraph says about the possible effects of evaluation on teaching can be applied to any specific activity which affects teaching practices. Our aim should be to have inquiries and actions which lead to the enhancement of learning.

The relationship between teaching and learning is a very old problem as well as a current one. In my conversations with faculty members these past two years, much anxiety has been expressed about the validity of many teaching practices. Do such practices result in learning? Does what the professors do make any difference? Robert Dubin and Thomas C. Taveggia in *The Teaching-Learning Paradox,* after reviewing four decades of research conclude: "The old ideas about pedagogy at the college level are simply wrong. . . . We cannot claim superiority for any among different teaching methods used to convey subject content to the student. . . . There is no measurable difference among truly distinctive methods of college instruction when evaluated by student performance on final examinations."[2] There are, of course, fundamental questions about the precise meaning of the terms *measurable differences* and *truly distinctive methods.* We may also question the validity of using student performance on a final examination as an adequate measure of effectiveness of instruction. Dubin and Taveggia's work may indicate more about the limitations of the kind of research it reviews than about the effects of different kinds of instruction. Nevertheless such statements increase the profession's general uneasiness toward what it knows about teaching and strengthens suspicions about the part teaching actually plays in learning.

Another evidence of uneasiness about teaching is the zeal

[1] Eble, *Recognition,* p. 49.
[2] Eugene, Ore.: University of Oregon, 1968, pp. vii, viii, 35.

with which "behavioral objectives" have been taken up in public schools and colleges. One can hardly take exception to emphasis on the need for teachers to set forth their instructional objectives as precisely as possible and to try to achieve those objectives. The difficulties with this approach are considerable and may become more marked if we insist upon seeing the effect of all kinds of instruction for a variety of students in terms of observable behavior. Changing the term to *performance objectives* removes some of the limitations imposed by the word *behavior,* but the emphasis still falls heavily on measurable effects induced by instruction. The connection between definitions of instructional objectives and accountability is natural.

Public distrust of education, rooted no doubt in the parallel rise in student unrest and the costs of public and private higher education, may strengthen general suspicions toward the effectiveness of teaching and toward the teaching art itself. In addition, the interest of the public and of at least part of the profession has been drawn away from teachers and toward technology. Many administrators saw television as a way of reducing costs by reducing the major item of expense, the employment of individual teachers. Televised instruction has by now become commonplace in large institutions for certain specific kinds of teaching and teaching situations. Computer-assisted instruction and self-paced, individualized instruction facilities are sweeping applications of technological devices to tasks formerly consigned solely to teachers. As yet, prophetic claims for this type of instruction have fallen far short of fulfillment. George E. Arnstein, reviewing Ralph W. Gerard's book *Computers and Education* (McGraw-Hill, 1967), writes: "Computer-based instruction is not now economically competitive, and every news release heralding the teacherless campus of the future, with cathode-ray tubes and individual carrels for all, deserves to be viewed with continuing suspicion."[3] Currently, there is probably more public suspicion of the teacher, however, than there is of teaching technology.

Professors cannot lightly set these matters aside. The need to find out about teaching effectiveness, to define what the teacher

[3] *Educational Record,* 1968, *49*(2), 239–240.

is trying to do, and to ascertain whether or how well teachers are succeeding, the need to use all the assistance technology can provide, should press upon the teaching profession. Although teachers are probably as reluctant as other human beings to embrace changes which threaten a satisfactory existing condition, their resistance is not necessarily or purely defensive. Many teachers I have encountered are anxious about their own usefulness in the eyes of the students. Some question the specific usefulness of the positions they occupy with respect to society. These anxieties about teaching practices often flow from different conceptions of what a university professor should be.

Right now, the conception of the professor as a facilitator of the student learning has much support. The students' desires to have some say in the teaching-learning process and some faculty members' dislike of the truthsayer's role find mutual support in this concept. Recently, I heard a young professor speak eloquently about this conception of a teacher, using a passage from Soren Kierkegaard to describe it:

> It is so on the stage, as you know well enough, that someone sits and prompts by whisper; he is the inconspicuous one, he is and wishes to be overlooked. But then there is another, he strides out prominently, he draws every eye to himself. For that reason he has been given his name, that is, actor. He impersonates a distinct individual. In the skillful sense of this illusory art, each word becomes true when embodied in him, true through him— and yet he is told what he shall say by the hidden one that sits and whispers. No one is so foolish as to regard the prompter as more important than the actor. Now forget this light talk about art. Alas, in regard to things spiritual, the foolishness of many is this, that they in the secular sense look upon the speaker as an actor, and the listeners as theatergoers who are to pass judgment upon the artist. But the speaker is not the actor—not in the remotest sense. No, the speaker is the prompter. There are no mere theatergoers present, for each listener will be looking into his own heart. The stage is eternity, and the listener, if he is the true listener (and if he is not, he is at fault), stands before God during the talk.[4]

[4] *Purity of Heart Is to Will One Thing,* D. V. Steele (Tr.) (New York: Harper & Brothers, 1938), p. 180.

165

The passage is worth any teacher's thoughtful contemplation. The role described might be ideal for some teachers. But like most definitions of the ideal teacher, it is as limiting as it is attractive. Another conception is advocated by William Arrowsmith:

> If I had a campus to play with, my first step would be to plant there, at any price, the six or seven charismatic teachers of my acquaintance; their collective *aretē* would, I am convinced, create a curriculum that would truly, explosively, educate. But it is these men we must have, regardless of their academic pedigrees—prophets, poets, apocalyptics, scientists, scholars, intellectuals, men who sprawl across departmental boundaries, who will not toe the line, individuals as large as life, irrepressible, troublesome and—exemplary.[5]

Both of these men are urging special kinds of teachers, the first succeeding by the force of his invisible guidance, the other by force of a vital and active presence. Either role, carried out with awareness as well as conviction, is superior to the ordinary teaching functions as I have observed them carried out in classrooms I have visited. But both concepts, it seems to me, fail to recognize the diversity of teaching styles that can and should characterize the profession. These two examples afford a kind of continuum of teaching styles from the style which makes the least of the teacher as public performer to that which makes the most. Uneasiness about the teacher's role may relate to these extremes.

Something about the teacher's fundamental position as scholar militates against his being a public performer. The necessary isolation of the scholar, his attachment to books and ideas, his loyalty to his subject, the necessity for objectivity and detachment, and the suspicions of a vulgar public may set him against declamation and display. Whatever the causes are, they work against charisma. Truly charismatic teachers probably emerge without or despite efforts at developing them. Of greater importance are attempts to incline young teachers still developing their styles to respect the wholeness and vitality central to Arrowsmith's conception of the teacher. The possibilities of making a marked personal impress are not re-

[5] "The Future of Teaching," p. 63.

stricted to charismatic personalities. But no teacher is likely to develop a style worthy of emulation if he or she has doubts about the validity of the teacher's role. There is considerable hostility at present toward personality in teaching. This hostility is justified in part. The teacher does have students at his mercy, so to speak, and he can inflict his personality upon them in disregard of subject matter or of the students' learning. But we should also be hostile to teaching that has no presence, that does not embody any image of a developing, learning human being. "I am not suggesting that teachers must be heroes or great men," Arrowsmith writes, "but they must understand greatness and desire it for themselves and others."[6]

The other model of teacher, Kierkegaard's prompter, is attractive to many young scholars. Like the charismatic model, it too arouses professional resistance. The actor in many teachers will not be easily pushed off the stage. If he is a competent and honest actor, it would be a mistake for him to depart. The self-effacing teacher can hide professional weaknesses as easily as the self-displaying one exposes his to the public. A quiet, unobtrusive presence may not offer even the bare minimum of guidance, motivation, or engagement with subject matter necessary to learning. Some young teachers are capable of seeing the class as a living organism, something that grows and declines in mysterious ways independent of the teacher's will or desires. At that point, it seems to me learning is left too much to itself. The teacher's admirable intent of giving first importance to the students' learning may become an abdication of basic responsibilities.

Fortunately, the extremes are not the only possible effective teaching styles. Between them lie many ways in which university teachers can carry out a highly valuable function. There is a place for teachers competent in transmitting information or developing skills, in imposing discipline or inspiring imagination. As generosity is favorable to developing the individual teacher's effectiveness, so it is favorable to recognizing different kinds of effective teaching within an institution. The present urge to break away from instructional modes has created new ways of learning which can be incorporated

[6] *Ibid.,* p. 61.

into teaching styles. Cooperative group processes, including group projects and examinations, satisfy one kind of teaching personality. Independent study with shrewd guidance and tutorial encounters satisfies another type. Living-learning arrangements can usually draw faculty participation for at least limited periods. Gaming, encounter, and confrontation, if not taken too seriously, add useful elements of play and reality to formal instruction. Teaching accompanied by experience satisfies the urges of some teachers and students to be doing and learning at the same time. The presence of these and other possibilities suggests that teaching is far from obsolete, however widely some teaching styles may depart from traditional forms.

The variety of teaching styles should be matched by the variety of individuals engaged in teaching. Both types of variety are necessary for the diversified student body increasingly characteristic of colleges and universities. The need for variety in teaching, teachers, and teaching styles is complicated in many institutions by the fact that teaching is only a part of the university's expectations of faculty members. It is encouraging that both the Scranton report[7] and the report of the Assembly on University Goals and Governance[8] reaffirm teaching and learning as the central function of the university. Endorsement of this position, however, will not solve many of the problems of recognizing and rewarding various kinds of teaching. It is important to identify the necessities of instruction, to clarify the worth attached to these necessities, and to judge and reward competence in teaching. If this were done, some of the values the university acts upon might be more carefully considered, and teaching might be seen as more than just one type of activity.

Consider the nature of instruction in many colleges and universities. Much of this instruction could be described as an orderly presentation of facts or principles which add up to a recognizable segment of a body or sequence of knowledge. It seems to me, however, that this is teaching of a fairly low order. One can probably distinguish fairly justly between teaching of this type done poorly—

[7] P. 20.
[8] *A First Report* (Cambridge, Mass.: The American Academy of Arts and Sciences, 1971), pp. 6–7.

disorganized, unsequenced, uninformed—and this style of teaching done well. But the value of this kind of teaching, even at its best, often escapes scrutiny. It seems quite possible that both professors and students might accept transmission of knowledge as desirable, might accept the lecture method as the most efficient method of transmitting knowledge, might even acknowledge the competence of individual lecturers and still be dissatisfied with the results. It is just this kind of instruction in which the teacher could most easily be replaced through technology.

A basic distinction can be made between teachers engaged chiefly in this kind of instruction and teachers who act as catalytic agents, who may actually effect changes in their students. The metaphor is not exact, for the professor, though he is a catalytic agent, would change too. It is the teacher's ability to be changed and to reflect these changes in subsequent encounters that distinguishes teaching of this kind. Because of his greater knowledge, experience or skill, the teacher has a clearer idea than his students of where their mutual inquiries may take them. At the same time, and despite his greater depth and breadth, he remains open and keeps his students open to avenues neither may have anticipated. Such teaching has as a minimum qualification the extension of knowledge beyond merely imparting information in traditional ways.

I do not intend to imply that college and university teachers fit only into these two categories. At times, all teachers need to communicate simple information and work with basic skills. Courses or subject matters may favor one kind of teaching over another although teaching can usually rise above the constraints placed upon it by the nature of a course. If we attach more importance to teaching which energizes students, teaching in which his whole development is involved, we profitably enlarge our concept of what education should be.

Teaching of this kind matters and will continue to matter. Part of a teacher's function is to disclose to the student things worth knowing, caring about, and giving part or all of their lives to. If the teacher has never thought of the importance of his role and finds himself with students who do not seem much interested in the subject matter he is professing frustration is bound to arise. But few subjects in any period of time argue their worth unaided. The teacher who takes offense because current students fail to recognize the worth of his teachings may be the real offender for never having persuasively argued their worth.

Teachers who feel teaching is losing effectiveness may be reacting to a diminishing of their own authority. Professors are not alone in this respect; parents, public officials, police, traditions, institutions—all have lost authority. American ideals have always had a strain of resistance to authority. The general emphasis in American higher education upon developing citizens capable of free choice and independent action also speaks against authority. The teacher who needs to demonstrate authority is likely to be uncomfortable in the present atmosphere. This does not mean teaching is becoming obsolete. It may mean that teachers still cling to the ideal of a student who is more tractable, less troublesome, and more respectful toward authority than the ones they are currently teaching.

But authority can be perceived of in a way in which the personal needs of the teacher play a small part. Authority which works best for the teacher and for the student is authority freely acknowledged by the student and lightly held by the teacher. Authority is not invested in the teacher at all. A teacher can assume the posture Whitehead advocates, "that of an ignorant man thinking," without fear of debasing his office or limiting his effectiveness. Authority resides in learning itself. As it affects a classroom teacher, it resides in the learning he and his students are engaged in. Authority resides in the conduct of the teacher whose relationship to learning brings acknowledgment that he knows some things of value which deserve attention. Authority resides in the teacher's acknowledgment of the common ignorance which all share. This type of authority moves students not to rivalry but to emulation; not to obstinacy but to willingness to examine one's own premises; not to carrying out of assignments but to sharing in responsibilities.

On the subject of authority, as on other important subjects, Gilbert Highet's observations have not lost their currency:

Nor do the young like authority. They are natural anarchists. They would prefer a world of unpredictable disorder, without duties or responsibilities. Such a world is impracticable now. So the young must be taught to respect the principle of authority, and if they do not learn it in school they will find it very bitter to learn later. A subsequent duty of their teachers will be to teach them to distinguish beween different types of authority, to choose the good and reject the bad. Only a determined teacher can teach them the first lesson. If he is both determined and wise, he can teach them both.[9]

Later he observes, "authority without persuasion, the worst method of teaching."[10] The teacher's power to persuade depends in one large part upon the wholeness of his commitment to teaching and, in another, upon how well he gets across that commitment to his students.

The rejection of authority is as basic and as long established as the assertion of authority. Jesus, Oedipus, King Lear—the world's history, myth and story endlessly chronicle rebellion and offer the means by which one may develop a wiser understanding of the phenomenon. The rejection of authority which makes teaching difficult is heightened by students' resistance to the particulars of learning. In any roomful of students, the degree of resistance will vary greatly. With some students, resistance is certain to be intense. Though learning is pleasurable, the work of learning— concentration, repetition, and application—naturally arouses resistance. Overcoming that resistance has always been central to the teacher's job.

The exaggerated stances of a minority of students and institutional arrangements which separate teaching from learning, scholarship from teaching, student from teacher, and teacher from teacher may make college and university teachers feel a hopelessness that neither the times nor a longer perspective toward learning justifies. Teaching has never been easy. If certain conditions of the past decade have made it seem so, it is a very healthy sign that members of the profession are becoming personally aware of the demands teaching makes upon them. Teaching of sorts can be done as a diversion, a welcome and occasional relief from striving after more important accomplishments. Such teaching, appearing as an

[9] *The Art of Teaching* (New York: Knopf, 1950), p. 67.
[10] *Ibid.,* p. 268.

occasional motif in a varied pattern of learning, may work no great harm. But adopted as the general attitude or as the common practice of those professors who set the academic tone, it demeans the importance of teaching and the necessary skills great teaching demands. Perhaps the difficulties of reaching students now result from habits developed when teaching seemed so easy.

Some teachers may ponder the questions: "what am I doing wrong?" and "am I really doing right?" because of the shift of students away from ideals of competitive success. Teaching, it must be admitted, has placed reliance on these ideals. Grades and objective testing have worked as motivating factors because they defined academic success in fairly simple ways and because they were connected with tangible competitive rewards. Admission to a desirable school, scholarships, honor societies, and admission to graduate school all depend heavily on the grade point average. Grading on a curve has probably been the most common grading practice. Higher education has seemed to operate on a scarcity principle, that there can only be so many admitted to a given school, that a small percentage of the graduating class can be elected to honor societies, and that a limited number of A's, more B's, a lot of C's, and sufficient D's and F's are necessary to preserve standards. This system seems very reasonable in the context of American society. If we remove the barriers to competing, competition will make sure that the cream still comes to the top.

This is a simplistic philosophy for a society or for an educational system. It is so fundamental to the operations of the educational system, however, that modification of it in any respect seems to some faculty members not only a challenge to the authority of the teacher but a way of taking the necessary tools of his trade from him. Right enough, modification does threaten to take away both handles of simple motivation: rewards for those who succeed and failure for those who don't.

Students are right when they point out the punitive aspects of grading. The F grade does more than deny a person credit for a required course. It makes him repeat the course and records his failure in the permanent record. Punishment for failure is the harsh edge of competitive enterprise, tempered (through bankruptcy laws)

172

in the commercial aspects of American society, but only now being modified in the universities.

The modification of grading may seem like a small reform but I think it is evidence of a shift in attitude that both faculty and students share. The new attitude is in part a response to the ever-increasing mechanization of teaching and uneasiness about the accuracy and fairness of grading. The new attitude is also a challenge to competition as the only way learning can proceed. Teachers find themselves in a curious bind when they urge the student to learn for learning's sake and then surround his learning with grades and exam scores. The fact that custom and the teacher's ease support an idealistic regard for learning and a marketplace approach to grades probably accounts for the durability of both. Teachers may now be willing to move with the students and work to give up reliance on competitive measures as the only way to foster learning. Students may have an overly romantic idea of the ease of learning and of the beneficial effects of eliminating competition. But the faculty, constrained by university traditions and regulations, drawn into teaching in a competitive framework, and facing competition within their own practices, need to make conscious efforts to see the truth in the students' view.

Another way in which teaching may seem to be losing its point for faculty and students is through the loss of simple pleasures in learning. The increased emphasis upon scholarship, the support of research, the tendency to make professional training the central purpose of every discipline, have brought more satisfactions to professors than to undergraduate students. I am not talking here just about major university centers where students are in a special kind of pressure cooker. I am talking about broader effects of the professional emphasis. The style of scholarly study is set by disciplinary associations and by graduate schools. Highly developed methodologies of research fasten on all subjects. In small and large colleges, for example, there is a passion for meticulous analysis of texts in all humanistic disciplines. Literature, a subject which was once central to general education, to which the widest range of human responses, including joy, could be expected, has become primary and secondary material for scholarship. Objects falling under formal study seldom rise to comedy. What may have been comic becomes solemnized through the scholarly process. The teacher, pressed by the institution to be productive and visible, by the public to be efficient and accountable, is too busy to pause for laughter. These are admittedly serious times. Admonitions come from all that the university must grapple with serious problems. Exhaustive studies of student unrest seldom note the amount of genuine play involved in campus confrontations. Faculty members have a difficult time even recognizing a student put-on. The put-on, a chief form of humor this past decade, is covert humor. It is both popular and easy in the university because of the seriousness with which academicians and future academicians go about their work.

None of this is meant to deny the seriousness of confrontations at Berkeley, Columbia, Kent State, Jackson State, and elsewhere. In some ways, however, one could argue that a partial cause of the tragedies at Kent and Jackson State was the utterly serious intent of the troops that carried out the deadly action. This discussion is not intended to imply that the pursuit of knowledge is not a serious pursuit. Yet, teaching is the very act that should bring out the comedy of life. Instead, the diligent graduate student turned professor academizes everything within his grasp. Were some joy restored to teaching, fewer teachers and students would feel the sense of weariness that arises from the vanity of serious effort.

Finally, some current practices of teaching may add to teachers' feelings of obsolescence. The very speed at which times change, the rate at which things wear out, the rapid shifts in fashion, opinion, manners, all have an impact. We do not mind looking back over a span of years and realizing we have fallen out of currency. We resent it when it happens daily.

Many teachers have mentioned that increased competition for the students' attention has reduced their satisfactions in teaching. The wash of professional entertainment, a good deal of it quasi-educational, the television newsmen, talk show hosts delivering monologues, panels of experts on important public questions, and the endless parade of personalities might make any teacher feel unequal to his task. The teacher could easily imagine that the impact of the media tends to nullify his own modest efforts.

174

Is Teaching Obsolete?

Questioning by students and colleagues of much of the academic tradition adds to a general feeling of insecurity. The tradition no longer stands as the unquestioned center of disciplinary studies. In almost all fields, old specialties are losing currency; new ones are coming in. Students are not the only ones who switch their interests; scholars have had to reconcile themselves to changes within their disciplines. Changes in academic style make their mark upon faculty as well as upon students.

From every quarter, the academic community seems pressed by demands for change. Current pressures come on top of a period which, for most faculty members, was one of constant adaptation to change. Immediately after World War II, there was a race to meet the flood of incoming students. After that, or along with it, it was necessary to acquire physical facilities and work out designs to consolidate growth that had been ruled largely by expediency. Having, perhaps, mastered growth and followed the planners who saw a primary need to train more, if not better, college and university teachers, the faculty member, now firmly established in graduate work, faces angry and anxious Ph.D. candidates who cannot find jobs.

The many considerations that arise if one takes seriously the question, "Is teaching obsolete?" emphasize my conviction that teaching matters and that the seventies offer great opportunities for teachers. The building of graduate institutions and the development of graduate research and scholarship may have reached, for a time, a point of consolidation. Public financing and professional responsibility may now shift to undergraduate education. The concluding conference of the project on renewing undergraduate teaching perceived the shift taking these forms:

> Faculty members should be urged to critically examine their teaching behavior. They should also be provided with a variety of resources to support and encourage their efforts.
>
> Colleges and universities should provide institutional support for the creation of alternative teaching environments by: (a) Identifying and creating change agents among members of the faculty, administration, and student body. (b) Assisting change agents in

developing experimental programs. (c) Appointing members to curriculum and course of study committees who are interested in and supportive of experimental environments. (d) Developing a constituency in the institution that will accept and support alternative teaching environments. Especially important in this constituency are deans, department chairmen, senior faculty members, and student leaders. (e) Providing funds and making budgetary adjustments so that new programs can go forward without sacrificing vital interests of departments and schools within the institution. (f) Rewarding student and faculty participation in programs to create alternative environments.

While the more general and abstract aspects of education—theory, description, and observation—continue to have a central role, there is a need to combine these general, abstract aspects with concrete and active aspects, such as projects, productions, and outputs.

The dominant concept of curriculum locks people, faculty and students, into routines. The need is for more programs of short duration, more flexibility. One important way to achieve this is to allocate more resources within institutions to teaching and learning situations negotiated by the participants, including student-initiated courses. The curriculum should not be viewed as largely static, but as normally in flux.

The academic calendar at present is a barrier to flexibility and to certain types of activities. The entire calendar year should be utilized. Rigidities of the academic calendar should be reduced so that activities of greatly varying duration can be accommodated. There should be less pre-programming of activities by teachers and students. Time should be placed in reserve to be used for the creation of new activities during the year as occasion, ideas, and events bring new interests to the surface and new groupings of resources together.

The model in which academic progress for the students and workload for the faculty is measured in units of time—credits, units, hours—obstructs flexibility. The movement should be away from time measures to competence measures administered as much as possible on demand. Generally, competence should mean demonstrated ability for independent performance.

Structural features which limit the opportunity for collaborative teaching efforts should be removed.

Is Teaching Obsolete?

Expertise in a particular subject matter should not be a prereq-
uisite to teaching that subject. General teaching competence, extensive educational background, interest in pursuing a subject or
question, and willingness to do so should be considered sufficient
for a teacher to undertake a particular activity.

Our answer to the question "Is teaching obsolete?" is a firm
no. The times, in fact, may be favorable to teaching, and may provide more opportunities for a variety of teaching styles. I think college teachers who find the profession most rewarding in the years
ahead may be those who see themselves as agents for learning,
catalysts for students' development. Such teachers will regard motivation as their primary responsibility, and will push themselves
and their institutions for means through which motivated students
can further their learning. Stimulation of the student will be as
much of the imagination as of the intellect. The teacher's aim, if
he chooses to define a single goal, will tend more toward developing
understanding than toward imparting knowledge. Students will
push beyond routinely acquiring information and skills; they will
insist that learning be conjoined with doing, and the teacher will
help make that conjoining possible.

The successful teacher will function as a model but not
necessarily as the model of the professional scholar. Large numbers
of these teachers may not be professional scholars at all. They may
be college teachers only for a period of time. Professional scholars
or not, these teachers will make their presence an integral part of
their teaching. This presence will not be a mere parading of vanities,
or exploitation of personalities; it will proceed out of a need to afford students models. The teacher's personality is not as important
as his character. If teachers despair of building character in students, they should not despair of building it in themselves.

The teacher will be a committed citizen of the world as well
as a member of the scholarly community. His loyalties, commitments, and avowals will be open, not wished or thrust upon students but visible as any citizen's loyalties, commitments, and avowals
should be open to inspection. He will be a political person in a way
that will resist politicization by taking his day-by-day political responsibilities as seriously as he takes his scholarly duties.

177

I have emphasized virtues of teaching rather than command of a subject matter. The one need not exclude the other. Beginning with virtue, a teacher can be expected to equip himself adequately in the particulars of having a subject to teach. He will, as a matter of similar importance, develop the art of teaching. He will also embody some visible imperfections of a different kind than are commonly attributed to teachers today. He will be ignorant of many things and rather than cover up his ignorance he will betray it because he will choose not to mind his own business, because he will teach things he has not devoted a lifetime to, and because he will remain interested in his students' and his own education. He will be a trifler at times, and a giver of attention to some of the petty details of existence which may humanize his scholarship. He will have shortcomings in respect to the ordinary necessities of high-level instruction: a less than oracular voice, perhaps, an inability to quite reach complete classifications or exact orderings, a less than superb command of dates, a shaky hand at the blackboard. His virtues will be tempered with vices which may keep him close to students and learning. Such teachers make a difference, and such teaching is never obsolete.

EPILOGUE

Professors as Teachers

If college teaching is to be improved, diverse forces must change both attitudes and practices. The project has emphasized affecting faculty members, administrators, and institutional structures in ways favorable to teaching. I have found wide support for a belief that the values dominant in higher education fail to give adequate support to teaching. But few concrete suggestions have been made about how to change these values. My own conviction is that a shift in values is most likely to come about in the graduate schools, the reward system, and in institutional structures for learning.

The graduate school is surely where a college professor's values are most firmly established. "The young faculty recruit," Allan Cartter writes, "is an impressionable person, and the two most important periods in his life are those that immediately precede and follow his getting the doctorate."[1] These years in which one might expect most to be done toward preparing him for a teaching career often provide very little help. The sorting processes of ad-

[1] "University Training and Excellence," in Lee, *Improving College Teaching*, p. 161.

179

mission and progress toward an advanced degree tend to reproduce existing faculty values and attitudes. The dominance of research is clearly a consequence of graduate education. And the narrowness of vision, the disdain for education, the reluctance to function as a teacher are ills attributable in large part to graduate training. Upgrading the preparation of college teachers in graduate schools is therefore fundamentally important not only to improving teaching but to refashioning higher education.

College teachers are no more mercenary than other American citizens. They may even be less. But in higher education, as in other enterprises, we get what we pay for. Any substantial alteration in graduate school values or programs will not come about without financial support. The teaching assistantship in research-oriented state universities furnishes a concrete example. Until institutions are willing to resist drawing upon this ready supply of cheap labor, graduate work and undergraduate teaching will both suffer. Unfortunately, there is little indication that institutions or outside agencies will provide more satisfactory financial support of basic undergraduate courses or of graduate students planning to become college and university teachers.

Within the college or university, the reward system can be affected by defining in ways favorable to teaching the policies and practices which determine appointments, promotions, and salaries. But equally important, it seems to me, is substantial financial support for teaching from the top of the university budget. Faculty development has been shamefully neglected. The power of departments strongly favors disciplinary values. Annual teaching awards, kind words about devoted teachers, even evaluation systems do little if tangible and continuing support is not provided for effective teaching.

The most necessary structural change within a university is the building of forces to offset prevailing structures which work against undergraduate instruction. The establishment of university professorships has been urged as one way to recognize the importance of teaching. In proposing such a countervailing force, William Arrowsmith writes: "Though this professorship is still an uncertain novelty, occupying a still undefined institutional position, it has usually come into existence because enterprising administrators felt the need for countering the effects of extreme departmental specialism."[2] University professors would exemplify teaching of extraordinary excellence. Their responsibilities and aims would be broader than those of a discipline or a department, concerned with education rather than with technical professional training. Their appointments would be university, not departmental, appointments, and they need not be permanent. Their salaries would come from the university, not the department, budget. Their numbers should be sufficient to affect the university community. The presence of large numbers of professors who had enjoyed or were enjoying broadly educational roles as university professors could work great changes in the character of an institution.

Such a departure from departmental and disciplinary structures might naturally lead to new ways of involving students and faculty in education. Learning might break away from the restricting effects of historical sequencing, disciplinary boundaries, and the confines of particular theory and methodology. The steady increase in free electives is reason enough for seeking attractive alternatives to present learning structures. The university's responsibility is surely not only to offer the student a great variety of courses but to offer several avenues by which degrees can be achieved. Foremost is the need for faculty and students to arrive at clusters of course work not governed primarily by present course packaging, credit-hour accounting, department majoring, and routine methods of instruction.

Within institutions and the profession, much needs doing to make information about teaching available. Faculty members know very little of what goes on outside their office doors. If that statement seems unduly severe, then they know very little outside the building they occupy or the college they teach in. To some degree, being uninformed is necessary to a professor's survival. His discipline, the department, the institution, the commercial enterprises on the fringe flood him with information. Nevertheless, I strongly propose that any institution which shelters hundreds of

[2] "The Future of Teaching," p. 69.

teachers and thousands of students needs a central place concerned with teaching and learning. I have in mind something as simple as a central source for gathering, selecting, and digesting information about teaching and getting that information into the hands of those —students, faculty, administrators—who can use it. Such a center should not be aimed primarily at research or be identified with a college or school of education. Ideally, it would involve an institution's best teachers in many disciplines serving in diverse ways for limited periods of time.

If such simplicity and diversity could be maintained, a national center could serve a similar purpose for the profession at large. One example of current neglect will suffice. At the present time, the profession lacks a comprehensive, up-to-date bibliography on college teaching, the basic research tool that exists as a matter of course in all disciplines. The Eells' annotated bibliography, *College Teachers and College Teaching*,[8] met this need in 1957. But because of the general neglect of teaching, this indispensable resource was discontinued after being carried forward to about 1964. Though the Educational Resources Information Center may, in time, fill this need, its publications do not yet provide an adequate bibliographical resource for college and university teaching. A national center for teaching is vital to this need and the related necessities of putting information to use.

As I completed my work, I was often asked, "Has college teaching improved?" and "Is college teaching receiving more attention now than in the past?" None of us has many ways of judging whether teaching is better or worse now than it was at some previous time. The findings and recommendations of an AAUP committee studying the improvement of teaching in 1933 are not very different from those in this book. Such a similarity over so many years may affirm that, within the college and university structure, teaching is always in danger of being neglected, always in need of improvement. I sense a stronger interest in teaching on my own

[8] W. C. Eells, *College Teachers and College Teaching, an Annotated Bibliography* (Atlanta, Ga.: Southern Regional Education Board, 1957); First Supplement, 1959; Second Supplement, 1962; Third Supplement by M. L. Litton and W. H. Stickler, 1967.

campus today than existed in the sixties. Colleagues in most schools I visited express similar views. A shifting of attention to teaching may be in process as a means of redressing the imbalance between graduate and undergraduate education and as a recognition of economic and social needs.

Forces external to the university may also be causing a shift of emphasis. The growth in graduate education has been paralleled in the last decade by a remarkable expansion of public junior and community colleges. Concern for the rising costs of higher education may cause a falling off of financial support for both. In the competition for funds, broad training for the general public may be closer to the public's interest than graduate research in all the disciplines. The intensity of social problems—poverty and racism and the decay of the environment and the cities—may speak more to the need for broad educational and vocational programs than for professional academic preparation. The reduced market for college and university teachers and Ph.D.s outside the university has already caused cutbacks in admissions to advanced degree programs. The reduction may bring a higher proportion of faculties into undergraduate programs. In these related facts may lie the most realistic hopes for substantial improvement in college teaching.

This book necessarily expresses itself in a single author's words, and I take full responsibility for what has been said. The discussions in various chapters, however, draw heavily upon the work of conference groups involving many individuals holding many shades of opinion. Though this book cannot hope to do full justice to their views, it intends to reflect their strong and continuing interest in teaching.

Participants in the conferences on evaluation and career development are listed in *The Recognition and Evaluation of Teaching* and *Career Development of the Effective College Teacher*. Participants in the project's final conference at St. John's College, Santa Fe, were: Andrew Aguilar, CARISSMA, Commerce, California; Earnestine Beatty, psychology, University of Louisville; William Birenbaum, president, Staten Island Community College; Caroline Boiarsky, Peoria, Illinois; Laura Bornholdt, vice-president, The Danforth Foundation; J. Orrison Burgess, education, University of Saskatchewan Regina Campus; Lori Clarke, English, University of Utah; David Danelski, government, Cornell University; Donald S. Dean, chairman, biology, Baldwin-Wallace College; Benjamin DeMott, English, Amherst College; Richard Desmond, director, Center of Higher Education, Illinois State University; Roger Ekins, English, University of Utah; David C. Epperson, Center for Urban Affairs, Northwestern University; Howard Foster, physics and mathematics, Alabama A&M University; Jerry G. Gaff, Center for Research and Development in Higher Education, University of California at Berkeley; Harry D. Gideonse, chancellor, New School for Social Research; John Gillis, executive associate, Association of American Colleges; Gerald Grant, Experimental College Study, Harvard University; Milton Hildebrand, zoology, University of California at Davis; Robert Jespersen, assistant dean, College of Arts and Sciences, University of New Mexico; Elma Johnson, English, Flint Community Junior College; Catherine Klesney, University of Western Michigan; Edward K. Kraybill, engineering, Pennsylvania State University; Pressley C. McCoy, Redlands, California; W. J. McGlothlin, education, University of Louisville; Jim McManus, Occidental College; Sally Main, Stanford University; Lester J. Mazor, Henry R. Luce Professor of Law, Hampshire College; Neill Megaw, chairman, English, University of Texas; Charles Meinert, Bureau of College Evaluation, State Education Department, Albany, New York; Donald O'Dowd, chancellor, Oakland University; Floyd O'Neil, assistant director, Center for Studies of the American West, University of Utah; Joseph Palaia, Consortium of Professional Associations; Anthony Rachal, Jr., executive vice-president, Xavier University of Louisiana; T. M. Robertson, mathematics, Occidental College; Arthur Ruoff, College of Engineering, Cornell University; Wilma Schneidermeyer, University of Southern California; Michael Scriven, philosophy, University of California at Berkeley; Clarence Shelley, assistant dean of student personnel, University of Illinois; Edward Joseph Shoben, Jr., executive vice-president, The Evergreen State College; Jim Sutton, University of Iowa; Gregory C. Thompson, research associate, American Indian history, University of Utah; Robert Van Waes, associate secretary, American Association of

Epilogue: Professors as Teachers

University Professors; Frank Vattano, assistant academic vice-president, Colorado State University; Sister Mary Veronica, academic dean, Xavier University of Louisiana; William E. Vincent, associate secretary, American Association of University Professors; Edgar Whan, English, Ohio University; Robert C. Wilson, Center for Research and Development in Higher Education, University of California at Berkeley; Henry Yost, biology, Amherst College; Aurelia Young, music, Jackson State College.

Selected
Bibliography

ADELSON, J. "The Teacher as a Model." *American Scholar,* Summer 1961, 383–406.

AGASSIZ, E. C. (Ed.) *Louis Agassiz.* Boston: Houghton Mifflin, 1885.

ALLEN, D. C. *The Ph. D. in English and American Literature.* New York: Holt, Rinehart and Winston, 1968.

American Association of Junior Colleges. *Preparing Two-Year College Teachers for the '70's.* Washington, D.C., 1969.

American Association of University Professors. "Statement on Faculty Workload." In *AAUP Policy Documents and Reports.* Washington, D.C., 1971.

ARDEN, E. "A Solution to the Crisis in College Teaching." *Liberal Education,* October 1965, 419–26.

ARNSTEIN, G. E. Review of R. W. Gerard (Ed.), *Computers and education. Educational Record,* Spring 1968.

ARNSTEIN, G. E. *Design for an Academic Matching Service.* Washington, D.C.: American Association for Higher Education, 1969.

ARROWSMITH, W. "The Future of Teaching." In C. B. Lee (Ed.), *Improving College Teaching.* Washington, D.C.: American Council on Education, 1967, pp. 57–71.

Assembly on University Goals and Governance. *A first report.* Cambridge, Mass.: The American Academy of Arts and Sciences, 1971.

ASTIN, A. W. *The College Environment.* Washington, D.C.: American Council on Education, 1968.

ASTIN, H. S. *The Woman Doctorate in America: Origins, Career, and Family.* Russell Sage Foundation, 1969.

187

Selected Bibliography

AXELROD, J. (Ed.) *Graduate Study for Future College Teachers.* Washington, D.C.: American Council on Education, 1959.

AXELROD, J., FREEDMAN, M. B., HATCH, W., KATZ, J., AND SANFORD, N. *Search for relevance.* San Francisco: Jossey-Bass, 1969.

BALLIET, C. "Impressions of Changes." Unpublished manuscript. Springfield, Ohio: Wittenberg University, 1970.

BARZUN, J. *The American University: How It Runs, Where It Is Going.* New York: Harper and Row, 1968.

BASKIN, S. (Ed.) *Higher Education: Some Newer Developments.* New York: McGraw-Hill, 1965.

BAYER, A. E. *College and University Faculty: A Statistical Description.* Washington, D.C.: American Council on Education, 1970.

BERELSON, B. *Graduate Education in the United States.* New York: McGraw-Hill, 1960.

BERNARD, J. *Academic Women.* University Park: Pennsylvania State University Press, 1964.

BIRENBAUM, W. M. *Overlive: Power, Poverty, and the University.* New York: Delacorte Press, 1969.

BOLIN, J. G., AND MC MURRAIN, T. *Student-Faculty Ratios in Higher Education.* Athens, Ga.: Institute of Higher Education, University of Georgia, 1969.

BOWLES, F., AND DECOSTA, F. A. *Between Two Worlds: A Profile of Negro Higher Education.* New York: McGraw-Hill, 1971.

BRANDIS, R. "The Rehabilitation of University Undergraduate Teaching." *Educational Record,* Winter 1964, 56–63.

BRAWER, F. *Personality Characteristics of College and University Faculty.* Washington, D.C.: American Association of Junior Colleges, 1968.

BRICK, M., AND MC GRATH, E. J. *Innovation in Liberal Arts Colleges.* New York: Teachers College Press, Columbia University, 1969.

BRICKMAN, W. W., AND LEHRER, S. *Conflict and Change on the Campus: The Response to Student Hyperactivism.* New York: School and Society Books, 1970.

BROWN, D. "Personality, College Environments, and Academic Productivity." In N. Sanford (Ed.), *The American College.* New York: Wiley, 1962, pp. 536–562.

BROWN, D. G. *The Market for College Teachers.* Chapel Hill: University of North Carolina Press, 1965.

BROWN, D. G. *The Mobile Professors.* Washington, D.C.: American Council on Education, 1967.

CAPLOW, T., AND MC GEE, R. *The Academic Marketplace.* New York: Basic Books, 1958.

CARMICHAEL, O. C. *Graduate Education: A Critique and Program.* New York: Harper and Row, 1961.

Selected Bibliography

CHESTER, D. N., AND ASSOCIATES. "The Organization of Graduate Studies and the Training of Graduates." *Universities Quarterly*, June 1964, 241–60.

CHICKERING, A. W. *Education and Identity*. San Francsico: Jossey-Bass, 1969.

CLARK, B. R. *The Distinctive College: Antioch, Reed and Swarthmore.* Chicago: Aldine, 1970.

CLARK, B. R. "Faculty organization and authority." In H. M. Vollmer and D. L. Mills (Eds.), *Professionalization*. Englewood Cliffs, N.J.: Prentice-Hall, 1966, 282–291.

The College Placement Council. *The College Graduate: His Early Employment and Job Satisfaction.* Bethlehem, Pa., 1969.

Commission on Undergraduate Education. *Biological Sciences News,* December 1969.

CONRAD, J. Preface to *The Nigger of the "Narcissus."* Harper and Row, 1951.

COOPER, R. "Improving college teaching and administration." In S. Baskin (Ed.), *Higher Education: Some Newer Developments.* New York: McGraw-Hill, 1965, 196–227.

COOPER, R. (Ed.) *The Two Ends of the Log.* Minneapolis: University of Minnesota Press, 1958.

CRAWFORD, S. C. "A University-Wide Program of Faculty Development." *Educational Record*, Jan. 1961, 49–53.

DAICHES, D. (Ed.) *The Idea of a New University: An Experiment in Sussex.* Cambridge, Mass.: M.I.T. Press, 1971.

DEAN, D. *Preservice Preparation of College Biology Teachers.* Washington, D.C.: Commission on Undergraduate Education in the Biological Sciences, 1970.

DEMERATH, N., STEPHENS, R., AND TAYLOR, R. R. *Power, Presidents and Professors.* New York: Basic Books, 1967.

DENNIS, L., AND KAUFFMAN, F. *The College and the Students.* Washington, D.C.: American Council on Education, 1966.

DENNIS, W. "Creative Productivity Between the Ages of 20 and 80 Years." *Journal of Gerontology*, 1966, *21*, 1–8.

DE VANE, W. C. "The Responsibility of the Modern Professor." *Liberal Education*, March 1961, 5–13.

DIBDEN, A. *The Academic Deanship in American Colleges and Universities.* Carbondale: Southern Illinois University Press, 1968.

DODDS, H. W. *The Academic President—Educator or Caretaker?* New York: McGraw-Hill, 1962.

DRESSEL, P. L., JOHNSON, F. C., AND MARCUS, P. M. *The Confidence Crisis.* San Francisco: Jossey-Bass, 1970.

189

Selected Bibliography

DRESSEL, P. L., AND PRATT, S. B. *The World of Higher Education: An Annotated Guide to the Major Literature.* San Francisco: Jossey-Bass, 1971.

DUBIN, R., HEDLEY, R. A., AND ASSOCIATES. *The Medium May Be Related to the Message: College Instruction by TV.* Eugene: University of Oregon, 1969.

DUBIN, R., AND TAVEGGIA, T. C. *The Teaching-Learning Paradox.* Eugene: University of Oregon, 1968.

DUNHAM, E. A. *Colleges of the Forgotten Americans.* New York: McGraw-Hill, 1969.

DUNLOP, J. T. (Chairman.) *Report of the Committee on Recruitment and Retention of Faculty.* Cambridge, Mass.: Faculty of Arts and Sciences, Harvard University, May 1, 1968.

DYKES, A. R. *Faculty Participation in Academic Decision Making.* Washington, D.C.: American Council on Education, 1968.

EASTMAN, A. M. (Ed.) *Proceedings of the Wingspread Conference on the Doctor of Arts Degree.* Washington, D.C.: Council of Graduate Schools, 1970.

EBLE, K. E. *Career Development of the Effective College Teacher.* Project to Improve College Teaching. Washington, D.C.: American Association of University Professors and Association of American Colleges, 1971.

EBLE, K. E. *The Recognition and Evaluation of Teaching.* Project to Improve College Teaching. Washington, D.C.: American Association of University Professors and Association of American Colleges, 1970.

EBLE, K. E. *Teaching, Research, and Professing.* Toledo, Ohio: Center for Study of Higher Education, University of Toledo, 1969.

ECKERT, R. E., STECKLEIN, J. E., AND SAGEN, H. B. "College Faculty Members View Their Jobs." *American Association of University Professors Bulletin,* December 1959, 513–528.

ECKERT, R. E., AND STECKLEIN, J. E. *Job Motivations and Satisfactions of College Teachers.* Cooperative Research Monograph No. 7. U.S. Government Printing Office, 1961.

ECKERT, R. E., WILLIAMS, H. Y., JR., AND ANDERSON, D. H. *The University of Minnesota Faculty: Who Serves and Why?* Minneapolis: University of Minnesota, 1970.

EELLS, W. C. *College Teachers and College Teaching, An Annotated Bibliography.* Atlanta, Ga.: Southern Regional Education Board, 1957; First Supplement, 1959; Second Supplement, 1962; Third Supplement by M. L. Litton and W. H. Stickler, 1967.

ERICKSEN, S. C. *Memo to the Faculty.* Ann Arbor: Center for Research on Learning and Teaching, University of Michigan, Vol. I—, 1963—.

Selected Bibliography

ERIKSON, E. H. *Childhood and Society.* New York: Norton, 1950.

ERIKSON, E. H. *Identity: Youth and Crisis.* New York: Norton, 1968.

ESTRIN, H. A., AND GOODE, D. *College and University Teaching.* Dubuque, Iowa: Wm. C. Brown, 1964.

EURICH, A. C. (Ed.) *Campus 1980: The Shape of the Future in American Higher Education.* New York: Delacorte Press, 1968.

EVERETT, W. *Graduate Education Today.* Washington, D.C.: American Council on Education, 1965.

FELDER, R. *Results of Questionnaire on Faculty Work Load.* Washington, D.C.: Educational Resources Information Center, 1968. ED 025 200.

FELDMAN, K. A., AND NEWCOMB, T. M. *The Impact of College on Students.* San Francisco: Jossey-Bass, 1969.

FEUER, L. S. *The Conflict of Generations: The Character and Significance of Student Movements.* New York: Basic Books, 1969.

FINGER, F. W. " 'Professional Problems': Preparation for a Career in College Teaching." *American Psychologist,* November 1969, 1044–49.

FISCHER, J. "Is There a Teacher on the Faculty?" *Harper's,* February 1965, 18, 20, 22, 24, 26, 28.

Fortune. "What They Believe: A *Fortune* Survey." January 1969.

FOWLER, J. M. "Progress Report of the Commission on College Physics for 1966–68." *American Journal of Physics,* November 1968, 1035–1067.

FREEMAN, R. B. *The Market for College-Trained Manpower: A Study in the Economics of Career Choice.* Cambridge, Mass.: Harvard University Press, 1971.

FURNISS, W. "Department and Faculty Profiles: An Aid to Judgment." *Liberal Education,* October 1963, 354–65.

GAFF, J. G., AND ASSOCIATES. *The Cluster College.* San Francisco: Jossey-Bass, 1970.

GAFF, J. G., AND WILSON, R. C. *The Teaching Environment.* Washington, D.C.: American Association of University Professors and Association of American Colleges, 1971.

GAMSON, Z. F. "Performance and Personalism in Student-Faculty Relations." *Sociology of Education,* 1967, 279–301.

GLEAZER, D. J., JR. *This Is the Community College.* Boston: Houghton Mifflin, 1968.

GORDON, O. *Profess or Perish.* Corvallis: Oregon State University Press, 1968.

GOULDNER, A. W. "Cosmopolitans and Locals." *Administrative Science Quarterly,* December 1957, 281–306.

"Graduate Training for College Teaching: A Panel Discussion." *AAUP Bulletin,* September 1960, 294–299.

191

GRAHAM, P. A. "Women in Academe." *Science,* September 25, 1970, 1284–1290.

GUSTAD, J. W. *The Career Decisions of College Teachers.* Atlanta, Ga.: Southern Regional Education Board, 1960.

GUSTAD, J. W. "Policies and Practices in Faculty Evaluation." *Educational Record,* 1961, *42,* 194–211.

HAMMOND, P. E., MEYER, J. W., AND MILLER, D. "Teaching Versus Research: Sources of Misperceptions." *Journal of Higher Education,* December 1969, 682–690.

HARCLEROAD, F. F. (Ed.) *Issues of the Seventies.* San Francisco: Jossey-Bass, 1970.

HARGENS, L. L. "Patterns of Mobility of New Ph. D.'s Among American Academic Institutions." *Sociology of Education,* 1969, 18–37.

HEFFERLIN, JB L. *Dynamics of Academic Reform.* San Francisco: Jossey-Bass, 1969.

HELBLING, R. "Deadwood in the Academic Forest." Paper presented to Conference on Career Development, Project To Improve College Teaching, Washington, D.C., 1970.

HEISS, A. *Challenges to Graduate Schools.* San Francisco: Jossey-Bass, 1970.

HIGHET, G. *The Art of Teaching.* New York: Knopf, 1950.

HILDEBRAND, M., AND WILSON, R. C. *Effective university teaching and its evaluation.* Berkeley: Center for Research and Development in Higher Education, University of California, April 1970.

HOBBS, M. T. "Teaching Loads in Selected Liberal Arts Colleges." *Liberal Education,* December 1966, 418–421.

HODGKINSON, H. *Institutions in Transition.* Washington, D.C.: Carnegie Commission on the Future of Higher Education, 1970.

HOYT, D. P., AND RAWSON, T. M. "Why Faculty Leave KSU." Research Report No. 1. Manhattan: Office of Educational Research, Kansas State University, December 1968.

INGRAHAM, M. *The Outer Fringe.* Madison: University of Wisconsin Press, 1965.

JACOB, P. E. *Changing Values in College.* New York: Harper and Row, 1957.

JAMES, W. *Memories and studies.* London: Longmans, Green, 1917, 329–347.

JENCKS, C., AND RIESMAN, D. *The Academic Revolution.* New York: Doubleday, 1968.

Johns Hopkins University. *The Course Guide.* Baltimore, April 1969.

JOSSEM, E. L. "The Challenge Renewed." *American Journal of Physics,* *36*(11), 1968.

Selected Bibliography

JOUGHIN, L. *Academic Freedom and Tenure*. Madison: University of Wisconsin Press, 1967.

KATZ, J., AND ASSOCIATES. *No Time for Youth*. San Francisco: Jossey-Bass, 1968.

KELLEY, W., AND WILBUR, L. *Teaching in the Community-Junior College*. New York: Appleton-Century-Crofts, 1970.

KENISTON, K. *The Uncommitted*. New York: Harcourt Brace Jovanovich, 1968.

KERR, C. *The Uses of the University*. Cambridge, Mass.: Harvard University Press, 1963.

KINNANE, M. "Attitudes of College Students Toward College Teaching as a Career." *Educational Record*, April 1962, 139–47.

KLAPPER, P. "The Professional Preparation of the College Teacher." *Journal of General Education*, April 1949, 228–44.

KLAW, S. *The New Brahmins: Scientific Life in America*. New York: Morrow, 1968.

KNAPP, R. "Changing Functions of the College Professor." In N. Sanford (Ed.), *The American College*. New York: Wiley, 1962, 290–311.

KNOX, W. D. "A Study of Relationships of Certain Environmental Factors to Teaching Success." *Journal of Experimental Education*, December 1956, 95–151.

KOEN, F., AND ERICKSEN, S. *An Analysis of the Specific Features Which Characterize the More Successful Programs for the Recruitment and Training of College Teachers*. Ann Arbor: Center for Research on Learning and Teaching, University of Michigan, 1967.

KRAYBILL, E. K. "Effective Teaching: Institutes for Engineering Teachers." IEEE Transactions on *Education*, June 1969, 85–88.

LAYTON, D. (Ed.) *University Teaching in Transition*. London: Oliver & Boyd, 1968.

LAZARSFELD, P. F., AND THIELENS, W. *The Academic Mind*. New York: Free Press, 1958.

LEE, C. B. T. (Ed.) *Improving College Teaching*. Washington, D.C.: American Council on Education, 1967.

LUTHANS, F. *The Faculty Promotion Process: An Empirical Analysis of the Administration of Large State Universities*. Iowa City: Bureau of Business and Economics Research, University of Iowa, 1967.

MC GEE, R. *Academic Janus*. San Francisco: Jossey-Bass, 1971.

MC GRATH, E. J. *The Graduate School and the Decline of Liberal Education*. New York: Teachers College Press, Columbia University, 1959.

193

Selected Bibliography

MC GRATH, E. J. *The Predominantly Negro Colleges in Transition.* New York: Teachers College Press, Columbia University, 1965.

MC GRATH, J. E., AND ALTMAN, I. *Small Group Research.* New York: Holt, Rinehart and Winston, 1966.

MC KEACHIE, W. J. "Research on Teaching at College and University Level." In N. L. Gage (Ed.), *Handbook of Research on Teaching.* Chicago: Rand-McNally, 1963, pp. 1118–72.

MANN, R. D., ARNOLD, S., BINDER, J., AND ASSOCIATES. *The College Classroom: Conflict, Change and Learning.* New York: Wiley, 1970.

Mathematical Association of America, Commission on the Undergraduate Program in Mathematics. *Qualifications for a College Faculty in Mathematics.* Washington, D.C., 1967.

MAYHEW, L. B. *The Literature of Higher Education 1971.* San Francisco: Jossey-Bass, 1971.

MEDSKER, L. L. *The Junior College.* New York: McGraw-Hill, 1960.

MELVILLE, H. *Moby Dick.* New York: Crowell Collier & Macmillan, 1962.

MILLER, G. E. *Teaching and Learning in Medical Schools.* Cambridge, Mass.: Harvard University Press, 1962.

MILLER, W. S., AND WILSON, K. M. *Faculty Development Procedures in Small Colleges: A Southern Survey.* Atlanta, Ga.: Southern Regional Education Board, 1963.

MILTON, O., AND SHOBEN, E. J., JR. (Eds.) *Learning and the Professors.* Athens: Ohio University Press, 1968.

MONSON, C. H., JR. "Teaching Assistants: The Forgotten Faculty." *Educational Record,* Winter 1969, 60–65.

MOONEY, W. T., JR., AND BRASTED, R. C. *A Report on the Education and Training of Chemistry Teachers for Two-Year Colleges.* Palo Alto, Calif.: Advisory Council on College Chemistry, Stanford University, 1969.

MORRIS, W. H. (Ed.) *Effective College Teaching.* Washington, D.C.: American Council on Education, 1970.

MUSCATINE, C. (Ed.) *Education at Berkeley.* Berkeley: Academic Senate, University of California, 1966.

NESS, F. *An Uncertain Glory.* San Francisco: Jossey-Bass, 1971.

NICHOLS, D. (Ed.) *Perspectives on Campus Tensions.* Washington, D.C.: American Council on Education, 1970.

NOWLIS, V. C., CLARK, K. E., AND ROCK, M. *The Graduate Student as Teacher.* Washington, D.C.: American Council on Education, 1968.

PACE, C. R. *College and University Environment Scales: Technical Manual.* Princeton, N.J.: Educational Testing Service, 1969.

Selected Bibliography

PARSONS, T., AND PLATT, G. M. *The American Academic Profession: A Pilot Study.* Cambridge, Mass.: Laboratory of Social Relations, Harvard University, 1968.

REICH, C. *The Greening of America.* New York: Random House, 1970.

"Report of the President's Commission on Campus Unrest (The Scranton Report)." *The Chronicle of Higher Education,* October 5, 1970.

REUSCH, N. R. *The Junior and Community College Faculty: A Bibliography.* Washington, D.C.: ERIC Clearinghouse for Junior College Information, 1969.

RICE, J. G. "The Campus Climate: A Reminder." In S. Baskin (Ed.), *Higher Education: Some Newer Developments.* New York: McGraw-Hill, 1965, 304–317.

RILEY, M. W., RONER, A., AND ASSOCIATES. *Aging and Society.* Vol. 1, An Inventory of Research Findings. New York: Russell Sage, 1968.

ROGERS, C. "The facilitation of significant learning." In L. Siegel (Ed.), *Instruction: Some Contemporary Viewpoints.* San Francisco: Chandler, 1967.

ROGERS, C. *Freedom to Learn.* Columbus, Ohio: Merrill, 1969.

ROSZAK, T. *The Making of a Counter Culture.* New York: Doubleday, 1969.

ROTHWELL, C. E., AND ASSOCIATES. *The Importance of Teaching: A Memorandum to the New College Teacher.* Washington, D.C.: Hazen Foundation, 1968.

RUDOLPH, F. *The American College and University.* New York: Knopf, 1962.

RUNKEL, P., HARRISON, R., AND RUNKEL, M. (Eds.) *The Changing College Classroom.* San Francisco: Jossey-Bass, 1969.

RUSSELL, J. D. "Faculty Satisfactions and Dissatisfactions." *Journal of Experimental Education,* December 1962.

Rutgers College Student Government Association. *Course and Professor Evaluation.* New Brunswick, N.J., Spring 1969.

SANFORD, N. *The American College.* New York: Wiley, 1962.

SANFORD, N. *Where Colleges Fail.* San Francisco: Jossey-Bass, 1967.

SANFORD, N. "Whatever Happened to Action Research?" *Journal of Social Issues,* 1970, 26(4).

SEELEY, J. "The University as Slaughterhouse." In *The Great Ideas Today 1969.* Chicago: Encyclopaedia Britannica, 1969.

SHUGRUE, M. "The National Study of English in the Junior College." *Junior College Journal,* June–July, 1969.

SMITH, G. K. (Ed.) *New Teaching, New Learning: Current Issues in Higher Education 1971.* San Francisco: Jossey-Bass, 1971.

SMITH, P. "Teaching, Research, and Publications as They Affect Academic Performance and Promotion." *Journal of Higher Education,* April 1961, 199–205.

Stanford University. *The Study of Education at Stanford.* Palo Alto, Calif., 1969.

STECKLEIN, J. E., AND LATHROP, R. L. *Faculty Attraction and Retention.* Minneapolis: Bureau of Institutional Research, University of Minnesota, 1960.

STERN, G. G. "Characteristics of the Intellectual Climate in College Environments." *Harvard Educational Review,* Winter 1963, 5–41.

Swarthmore College. *Critique of a College.* Swarthmore, Pa., 1967.

TAYLOR, H. *Students Without Teachers: The Crisis in the University.* New York: McGraw-Hill, 1969.

THOREAU, H. D. *Walden.* Cambridge, Mass.: Riverside Press, 1957.

THORNTON, J. W., JR., AND BROWN, J. W. *New Media and College Teaching.* Washington, D.C.: National Education Association, 1968.

TICKTON, S. (Ed.) *To Improve Learning: An Evaluation of Instructional Technology.* (2 vols.) New York: Bowker, 1970.

TROW, M., AND LIPSET, S. *National Surveys of Faculty and Students in American Higher Education.* Berkeley: University of California, 1969.

TUSSMAN, J. *Experiment at Berkeley.* New York: Oxford University Press, 1969.

VOEKS, V. *On Becoming an Educated Person.* 3rd edition. Philadelphia, Pa.: W. B. Saunders, 1970.

VREELAND, R. S., AND BIDWELL, C. E. "Classifying University Departments: An Approach to the Analysis of Their Effects upon Undergraduates' Values and Attitudes." *Sociology of Education,* 1966, 237–254.

WALLERSTEIN, I., AND STARR, P. (Eds.) *The University Crisis Reader: The Liberal University Under Attack.* Vols. I & II. New York: Random House, 1971.

WHALEY, W. G. (Ed.) *In These Times: A Look at Graduate Education with Proposals for the Future.* Austin: Graduate School, University of Texas, 1971.

WHITEHEAD, A. N. *Aims of Education.* New York: Mentor Books, 1949.

WILSON, R. C., GAFF, J. G., AND BAVRY, J. L. *Manual of Information for Faculty Characteristics Questionnaire.* Berkeley: Center for Research and Development in Higher Education, University of California, 1970.

WOODBURNE, L. S. *Faculty Personnel Policies in Higher Education.* New York: Harper and Row, 1950.

WORTHAM, M. "The Case for a Doctor of Arts Degree: A View from Junior College Faculty." *AAUP Bulletin,* Winter 1967, 372–377.

Index

197

Index

Index

Job: dissatisfactions of faculty, 159; satisfactions of faculty, 156–157, 158

Joy in learning, 89, 173–174

K

KENISTON, K., 76

KERR, C., 125

KIERKEGAARD, S., 165

Kinds of teachers and teaching, 168–169

KLAPPER, P., 6–7

Knowledge: advancement vs. dissemination of, 135–136; attitudes toward, 27–28, 132–133

L

Leadership 123, 125–126

Leaves, 110–111, 119, 130

Lecture classes: criticism of, 6–8; pervasiveness of, 4–6; relation to campus structures of, 11

LEE, C. B. T., 58

LUTHANS, F., 141

M

MC GEE, R., 107

MC KEACHIE, W., 36

M. PHIL. degree, 103, 105

Man-of-knowledge, 27–28

MANCALL, M., 104–105

Massachusetts, University of, 71

MELVILLE, H., 49

MILLER, W. S., 111

Motivation of learning, 177

Myths and stereotypes about teaching, 127–129

N

National Science Foundation, 100

Nature of university, faculty views of, 132–133

NEWCOMB, T. M., 74

North Carolina, University of, at Greensboro, 21

O

Optimum working conditions: concept of, 144–145; importance of salaries and benefits in, 154; project's work with, 2. *See also* Teaching environment

Oregon Program of Grants for the Improvement of Undergraduate Instruction, 116

P

Ph.D. *See* Doctorate

Phi Beta Kappa, 20

Placement of college teachers, 107–108

Pluralistic aims of higher education, 133–134

Preparing college teachers: criticism of, 98–101; guidelines for better programs, 101–102; importance of knowledge about teaching and learning, 31. *See* Ph.D. degree

Princeton University evaluation system, 71–72

Probationary period, 55–56

Project to Improve College Teaching, ix–xi, 1–3

Promotion policies, 141–142, 155

Prospective college teachers, 92–95; department responsibility for identifying, 95–96; selection process of, 94

Psychology of the teacher, 122

Public opinion of teaching, 153–154, 164

Publication, 135, 154–155

R

Recognition and Evaluation of Teaching, The, ix–x, 29, 36–37, 54, 70, 162–163, 183

REICH, C., 74

Renewing undergraduate teaching, 175–176

Report of Assembly on University Goals and Governance, 168

Research: conflicts with teaching, 26, 28–29, 131–132, 135, 156; in the humanities and social sciences, 138; judgments on value

Index

Index

V

Values in higher education, 132, 135–136, 140–141, 143, 179
Visiting classes: x–xi; 3; effects of, 3; method of, 2–3

W

Washington, University of, 71
Western Washington University, 116

WHITEHEAD, A. N., 36, 40, 86–87, 89–90, 170
WILSON, K., 111
WILSON, R., x, 144, 160
Women faculty, 27–28, 115
World War II, 84, 132, 175

Y

Youth culture, 74, 86, 88